health & vitality

cookbook

the vegetarian society's

health & vitality
cookbook

Lyn Weller
Foreword by Tina Fox

HarperCollins*Illustrated*

Editor: Heather Thomas
Photography: Chris Alack
Food stylist: Caroline Barty
Stylist: Sue Radcliffe
Index: Susan Bosanko

Colour origination by Colourscan Pte, Singapore
Printed and bound by Rotolito Lombarda, Italy

Acknowledgements

Lyn Weller would like to acknowledge the support of
everyone who helped to produce this book. In particular,
warmest thanks go to the staff of the Cordon Vert
Cookery School – Alison Verber for helping to test the
recipes, Maureen Surgey for manning the office during my
absences, and Deborah Clark and Rona Acton for their
support. Also, the staff of The Vegetarian Society for tasting
all the recipes and asking for more; their disappointment
when testing came to an end was most encouraging! Chris
Olivant for his advice and for editing the nutritional
information and The Institute of Brain Chemistry and
Human Nutrition for their nutrition software – Foodbase.
Thank you also to my partner Phil Pugh, for supporting me
throughout the process and for tasting some of the
recipes, too.

CONTENTS

FOREWORD
BY TINA FOX
CHIEF EXECUTIVE, THE VEGETARIAN SOCIETY

Whenever the phrases 'healthy eating' or 'low fat' are mentioned, I can almost hear the mental groan from an audience. All too often we consider that if food or drink is enjoyable or indulgent, it must be unhealthy and carry a price to pay, from the discomfort of indigestion to more serious health implications such as high blood pressure. However, you will discover just how wrong this misconception is by trying some of the mouth-watering recipes in this book.

Turn the pages and plunge yourself into the wonderful world of cuisine without consequence. In fact, the only outcome of eating these delicious dishes is that you will feel better for it. This is truly food without fear. The recipes have been tried and tested by the eager staff at The Vegetarian Society's headquarters, and you can be sure they pass the taste test with flying colours.

I have to admit to a few favourites of my own. For example, the Wild Mushroom Risotto on page 64 and the Wild Flower and Herb Salad on page 92 are a delicious combination that delight the tastebuds and provide an ideal balance of nutrients, and I defy anyone to eat the truly gorgeous Brandied Apricot Stacks on page 114 and feel they have missed out in any way.

Finally, an added bonus – by cooking the low fat and fun way described in this book, you may well live longer to enjoy the recipes!

INTRODUCTION
BY LYN WELLER
CORDON VERT MANAGER, THE VEGETARIAN SOCIETY

Health and Vitality – the key to a zest for life! Too often 'enjoyment' and 'healthy eating' are thought to be mutually exclusive, but with a balanced vegetarian diet both can be combined.

In this book I have set out to give you a variety of colourful and delicious recipes, which just happen to be healthy, too! Most of the recipes are suitable for everyday eating (and most are vegan), but there are one or two main dishes that I have flagged as particularly suitable for entertaining.

When we're busy we can get stuck in a rut and cook the same old recipes and stop thinking about what we are eating. I hope this book will give you some new ideas, and the menu suggestions will help you to put interesting combinations together. Most of the recipes are quick and easy to prepare (and many can be frozen), making them particularly suitable for a busy lifestyle. However, there are also some innovative recipes for those times when you want to spend a while in the kitchen, cooking for other people, too.

Each recipe has a basic nutritional breakdown so that you can see at a glance the amounts of nutrients you are gaining from each dish and choose your own menus.

The recipes have all been tested in The Vegetarian Society's own Cordon Vert Cookery School where we promote healthy vegetarian eating for everyone.

Eat vegetarian, eat healthily and eat well!

VEGETARIAN NUTRITION

Healthy eating is not about depriving yourself of the things you enjoy, but rather about achieving balance in your diet and educating your palate by making gradual changes towards healthier alternatives. Many people worry that if they stop eating meat and fish and adopt a vegetarian diet they may suffer some nutritional deficiency. However, a vegetarian diet can provide all the nutrients your body needs – from infancy to adulthood – and provided that you maintain a healthy balance there should be no cause for concern. In this introduction to basic vegetarian nutrition, you will discover good vegetarian sources of nutrients and some useful tips to help you achieve a healthy balance in your cooking without losing the flavours and textures that make food so enjoyable.

Research has shown that a vegetarian diet can have a beneficial effect on your health. In general, vegetarians are less prone to suffer from coronary heart disease, hypertension, obesity, various cancers, bowel disorders and diabetes. A vegetarian diet tends to follow the guidelines for healthy eating as laid down by NACNE (National Advisory Committee on Nutrition Education Report 1983), WHO (World Health Organisation 1990) and COMA (Committee on Medical Aspects of Food Policy, three reports COMA 1984, 1991 and 1994), all of which advocate a reduction in fat (particularly saturated fat), an increase in complex carbohydrates and fibre, and a decrease in sugar and salt in the diet. Current healthy eating advice recommends an increase in the consumption of fresh fruit and vegetables together with cereals and pulses. The 'five-a-day' campaign has promoted an increased awareness of the importance of fresh fruit and vegetables in the British diet. If you are a vegetarian, five portions a day should be easy to achieve.

WHAT ARE THE CONSTITUENTS OF A HEALTHY DIET?

There are five classes of nutrient required by our bodies for good health:

■ Protein
■ Fats
■ Carbohydrates
■ Vitamins
■ Minerals.

We also need fibre and water, which, although having no nutritional content, are necessary for the body to function properly. Most foods contain a range of nutrients but tend to be classified by the predominant one.

PROTEIN

A common question asked by budding vegetarians is 'Will I be able to obtain enough protein without eating meat?' The answer is 'Yes'! Proteins, to build and repair body tissue, are made up from amino acids. There are eight essential amino acids that we must obtain from food because our bodies cannot synthesize them.

Animal protein (meat, dairy products and eggs) contains amino acids in the right proportions, but they are available in plant proteins, too. A single plant source does not usually contain all eight amino acids in the right proportions, but a selection of different plant protein sources will ensure that your body's short-term pool of amino acids, which is drawn on through the day, is kept topped up.

Eating complementary proteins is no longer considered necessary as long as you eat a variety of foods through the day. Combining foods such as pulses and grains, or grains and nuts, will provide a complete protein. The classic examples in a vegetarian diet are beans on toast (pulse and grain), or muesli (grain, nuts and seeds).

If you take a quick look at your diet you should find that within any twenty-four hour period you have almost certainly consumed foods from more than one of these food groups. Vegetarians who consume dairy products (milk, cheese, yogurt, etc.) and eggs can obtain their protein quite easily, but even if you are not following a vegan diet it is unwise to rely on these products as they are also high in saturated fat. When becoming vegetarian, it's easy to fall into the trap of substituting eggs and cheese for meat and in so doing increase rather than decrease your saturated fat intake. Most of the recipes in this book are or can be dairy free and concentrate on the plant sources of protein which are also low in fat.

FATS

A healthy diet is low in fat, not 'no fat'. Some fat is necessary to keep our tissues in good repair, to manufacture hormones and to act as a carrier for the fat-soluble vitamins A,D,E and K. Fats are made up from fatty acids. Two of these (linoleic and linolenic acid) are termed essential fatty acids (EFAs) as our bodies cannot synthesize them. They occur widely in plant foods. (Vitamin E, a natural antioxidant, is also found in unrefined or cold pressed oils. It protects unsaturated fats and Vitamins A and C in the body as well as cell membranes.) The accepted recommendation is to reduce the amount of fat in our diet overall, and where we do eat fat, the proportion of unsaturated fats (mainly of vegetable origin) should be greater than saturated fats (animal products, coconut and palm oils) or hydrogenated vegetable oils.

CARBOHYDRATES

Carbohydrates provide the 'fuel' or energy for our bodies and enable us to metabolize proteins. They mostly come from plant foods.

■ Sugars are simple carbohydrates (monosaccharides) occurring naturally in all vegetable foods, milk and honey. Refined sugars provide sweetness but no nutritional benefit. All sugars play a contributory factor in obesity and dental decay. Unrefined sugars should contain some nutrients, making them preferable when sweetness is required. If you are eating processed foods you are likely to be consuming high amounts of sugar. For example, canned vegetables, baked beans and ready meals usually contain added sugar.

■ Complex carbohydrates or starches (polysaccharides) are found in cereals, grains and vegetables. Foods such as bread, pasta, rice, muesli, potatoes and parsnips are good sources of carbohydrates, and a healthy diet should contain plenty of these. Starches provide usable carbohydrate over a long period that keeps the blood sugar level smooth, and as they contain other nutrients their digestion means that vitamins and minerals are gradually released into the bloodstream along with the sugar that provides the energy.

■ Dietary fibre (non-starch polysaccharide) is the indigestible part of a carbohydrate food. Fibre helps to expel toxins and waste matter from the body and protects against diseases such as cancer of the colon and diverticular disease.

VITAMINS

Vitamins are chemicals required by the body in small quantities. Mainly the body cannot produce them for itself, so they have to be provided by the food we eat. There are two basic groups of vitamins:

- water soluble (B group, C and folic acid)
- fat soluble (A, D, E and K).

The body cannot store water-soluble vitamins so these are needed daily. Vitamins are easily destroyed during storage, processing or cooking. In general, the fresher and less processed the food, the higher the vitamin content. Water-soluble vitamins are destroyed by heat. They are often thrown away in the cooking liquid. Fat-soluble vitamins are more stable but are sensitive to light and air. If you can't obtain really fresh vegetables and use them up quickly, frozen vegetables are often better.

Vitamin A

Plants contain beta-carotene which the body turns into vitamin A, for a healthy skin, the growth of bones, resistance to infection and night vision.

B group

These convert proteins, fats and carbohydrates into energy, for the growth and repair of tissues and skin, for a healthy nervous system and for the production of red blood cells. The vitamin B12 present in plant foods is not readily available to humans and should not be relied on as a safe source. B12 is found in dairy products and fortified foods (e.g. some yeast extracts, soya milks, tofu, cereals and veggie-burger mixes).

Vitamin C

This is required to provide healthy skin, bones, teeth and gums, resistance to infection, wound healing, energy production and growth. It is found in citrus fruits, broccoli, spinach, peppers and berry fruits.

Vitamin D

This is necessary for the production of healthy bones and teeth. Vitamin D is found in dairy products and margarine. It is also produced by the body as a result of the action of sunlight on the skin.

Vitamin E

A natural antioxidant which protects vitamins A and C in the body as well as the cell membranes. Sunflower and other vegetable oils, wheatgerm, hazelnuts and avocados are all good vegetarian sources.

Vitamin K

This vitamin makes blood clot and prevents uncontrolled bleeding. It is found in spinach, cabbage and cauliflower. It is synthesized by the body from bacteria in the intestine. A deficiency is extremely rare.

MINERALS

Seven minerals are found in the body in large quantities. They are calcium, phosphorous, magnesium, sodium, potassium, chlorine and sulphur. All other minerals are required in tiny amounts (less than 100 mg per day) and are called trace minerals.

- Calcium, phosphorus and magnesium act together. Calcium, for the building and maintenance of strong bones and teeth, is particularly important during childhood, the teenage years and pregnancy. It is found in dairy products, leafy green vegetables, almonds, sesame seeds, dried fruit, pulses and fortified soya milk. Phosphorus and magnesium also help to maintain healthy bones and are used by the body for energy release. Widely found in plant foods, a deficiency is rare. Vitamin D acts with calcium, enhancing its absorption by the body.

- Sodium, potassium and chlorine are important in maintaining the body's fluid balance (water, blood and other fluids). Most people consume too much sodium which can lead to high blood pressure.

- Sulphur plays a role in some enzyme systems and a deficiency is rare.

- Iron is essential for the formation of haemoglobin which transports oxygen in the blood through the body. Iron deficiency is a common nutritional problem in a typical British diet, but vegetarians are no more prone to this than meat eaters. Vitamin C acts with iron to aid its absorption. It is advisable to combine foods that have a high vitamin C content with those containing a high level of iron. E.g. drinking a glass of orange with a meal aids the absorption of iron. The tannin in tea reduces the amount of iron absorbed and shouldn't be drunk an hour on either side of a meal. Leafy green vegetables, pulses, wholemeal bread, dried fruit and pumpkin seeds contain iron.

- Zinc is necessary for a healthy skin, immune system and resistance to infection as well as helping to heal wounds. Pumpkin seeds are one of the most concentrated sources.

HOW TO PLAN A HEALTHY DIET

Take a look at your current diet and analyse it to see where changes can be made. You can do this, element by element, by following the nutrient list above and asking yourself the following questions:

Proteins

■ Am I too reliant on dairy foods for the protein in my diet?

■ Can I replace some dairy-based meals with one using pulses, grain, nuts and seeds or soya products?

■ Am I taking protein from different plant groups at each meal or at least over the course of a day?

Fats

■ Am I eating too much fat?

■ Just what does I teaspoon or I tablespoon of oil look like?

■ Am I eating the right balance of fats or am I eating too much saturated fat?

■ Can the saturated fat in my diet be reduced and/or replaced with mono- or poly-unsaturates?

Carbohydrates

■ Am I eating enough starchy foods?

■ Can I reduce the amount of sugar in my diet, not only in drinks but by reducing the amount of processed foods consumed, too?

Vitamins and minerals

■ Am I eating five portions of fruit and vegetables a day? A piece of fruit at breakfast or in place of a sweet dessert can be beneficial.

■ Am I eating a wide range of fresh foods?

General

■ Am I eating a wide variety of food in each category or is my diet in a rut?

SOME TIPS TO HELP YOU

■ A squeeze of lemon or lime juice or a teaspoon of balsamic vinegar over salad gives a fat-free and simple salad dressing for everyday use.

■ Steam or stir-fry vegetables to minimize nutrient loss.

■ Eat fruit and vegetables raw where possible. A salad every day is a good rule.

■ Keep a food diary for a week or fortnight. Don't worry too much about quantities, but note down all the ingredients. Are you getting 'five-a-day' portions of fruit and vegetables, are you eating too much dairy food, could you reduce the fat, salt and sugar in your diet? Noting it all down for a short period gives you a guide to the constituents of your diet.

■ Use gomasio (10 parts roasted sesame seeds to I part salt, ground together), herb salt or a low-sodium 'salt' to reduce your sodium intake.

■ A glass of orange juice (Vitamin C) with a meal helps to increase the absorption of iron.

■ A healthy diet is low in fat but does not exclude fat altogether. The essential fatty acids are obtained from fat, and vitamins A, D, E and K are fat soluble.

■ Complex carbohydrates (starches) are better than sugar for energy. Eat lots of potatoes and pasta.

■ Measure the oil required in a recipe – don't just wave the bottle over the pan – you're bound to overestimate!

■ Cook mushrooms, onion and celery in a little vegetable stock with added shoyu instead of frying them.

■ The greatest vitamin content in fruit and vegetables is just under the skin. Buy organic produce where possible and scrub root vegetables rather than peeling them.

■ Buy your food as fresh as possible and eat it as soon as possible. Stored vegetables lose their vitamin content rapidly and cut vegetables even quicker.

■ Sprout your own beans and seeds in a jar – sprouting beans are highly concentrated in terms of nutrient content.

■ Try to cook your own and freeze an extra portion rather than buying ready meals and processed foods.

■ Beware of replacing meat with cheese. Cheese is high in saturated fat.

■ Chestnuts are low in fat (the only nut that is) so use these in preference to other nuts when possible.

■ Fresh fruit, vegetables and pulses are all good sources of fibre which is an essential part of your diet.

■ Make sure you are getting enough vitamin B12 by spreading your breakfast toast with a teaspoon of fortified yeast extract, or by using a fortified breakfast cereal and soya milk.

■ When buying food, always read the label. Many processed foods unexpectedly contain hidden fats and sugars.

A HEALTHY
START

*Left: Savoury breakfast rolls (page 30)
and Breakfast muffins (page 33)*

GRANOLA

If you think you don't like muesli, then try this recipe for granola (toasted muesli) as toasting the ingredients brings out their delicious flavours. This unusual breakfast cereal can be stored in an airtight container for a couple of weeks.

225 g/8 oz porridge oats
100 g/4 oz barley flakes
50 g/2 oz wheat flakes
50 g/2 oz sunflower seeds
100 g/4 oz roughly chopped mixed nuts
100 g/4 oz wheat germ
75 g/3 oz desiccated coconut
100 g/4 oz muscovado sugar
150 ml/¼ pint water
150 ml/¼ pint sunflower oil
1 teaspoon vanilla essence
½ teaspoon salt
100 g/4 oz luxury mixed dried fruits
     (pears, peaches, apricots, etc.), roughly chopped

■ Preheat the oven to 190°C/375°F/Gas Mark 5.
■ Mix the first eight (dry) ingredients together in a bowl. Whisk the water, oil, vanilla essence and salt together in a separate bowl. Add to the dry ingredients and mix well.
■ Spread out on a greased baking sheet and bake in the preheated oven for 30–60 minutes, turning occasionally until evenly browned (to taste).
■ Cool and then stir in the dried fruits. Store in an airtight container. Serve with skimmed, semi-skimmed milk or soya milk.

Serves 16

PER SERVING
■

310 kcals (1320 kj)
Protein 7 g
Carbohydrates 31 g
Fat 19 g
Fibre 3.5 g

SERVING SUGGESTION
■

A seasonal fresh fruit salad makes a wonderful breakfast. Mix a variety of fruits together in a serving bowl. Top with very low-fat natural fromage frais or low-fat yogurt or soya yogurt if desired, then sprinkle some granola over the topping and serve. Vary the fruits according to the season.

HOME-MADE SOYA
YOGURT WITH FRUIT PUREE

This recipe is also delicious if eaten unflavoured or with a few drops of vanilla essence added. You can use it as a topping for fruit and desserts (see page 14).

PER SERVING
■
66 kcals (274 kj)
Protein 5 g
Fat 3 g
Carbohydrates 5 g
Fibre 0.3 g

600 ml/1 pint soya milk (unsweetened)
4 tablespoons powdered soya milk* (optional)
1 tablespoon live natural soya yogurt
50 g/2 oz raspberries (or other fruit puréed)
15 g/½ oz icing sugar (optional)

To serve:
whole raspberries
sprigs of mint

■ Bring the soya milk to the boil in a saucepan. Remove from the heat and cool until tepid. Add the powdered soya milk and live yogurt and whisk well to blend.

■ Scald a large vacuum flask with boiling water to sterilize and warm it. Pour in the soya milk mixture. Replace the lid and keep in a warm place, undisturbed, overnight (5–8 hours). Turn out and refrigerate to firm the yogurt**.

■ Press the raspberries through a nylon sieve. Discard the pips. Stir in some icing sugar to sweeten, if liked.

■ Stir the raspberry purée into the yogurt and serve in glass bowls with extra raspberries and a sprig of mint to decorate.

Serves 4

* Available from health food stores. If you are unable to obtain it, you can make the yogurt without, but it will be runnier.

** Save 1 tablespoon of yogurt before adding the fruit, to use as a starter next time. Each time you make it, the yogurt will become thicker and better.

VEGAN

FRUIT CREPES

PER SERVING

■

316 kcals (1324 kj)
Protein 12 g
Fat 15 g
Carbohydrate 40 g
Fibre 4 g

For this very summery breakfast, you can vary the fruit in the filling according to what is in season. Strawberries with kiwi fruit make a pleasant change, whereas in the winter, orange and grapefruit can be used. Fresh fruit is a good source of Vitamin C.

50 g/2 oz plain white flour
50 g/2 oz gram flour, sifted
15 g/1/2 oz poppy seeds
300 ml/½ pint soya milk
pinch of salt
1 teaspoon sunflower oil
150 ml/5 fl oz natural soya yogurt
   (see page 15)

For the filling:

2 ripe bananas, chopped
juice of 1 lemon
50 g/2 oz ready-to-eat dried
   apricots, chopped
50 g/2 oz toasted almonds, chopped
1 teaspoon groundnut oil

To decorate:

1 teaspoon poppy seeds (optional)
thin slivers of lemon zest

■ To make the pancakes, blend the flours, poppy seeds, soya milk and salt in a blender or food processor. Leave to stand for 20 minutes.

■ Meanwhile, make the filling by mixing the bananas, lemon juice, apricots and almonds together.

■ Heat a little of the oil in a non-stick pancake pan. Use a 50-ml/2-fl oz ladle to measure the batter for each pancake. Pour the batter for one pancake into the pan, swirling it around to cover the base evenly. Cook until set and golden brown underneath, then flip the pancake over and cook the other side. Make 8 pancakes and layer to keep warm.

■ Fill each pancake with a couple of spoonfuls of the filling and fold into quarters. Arrange 2 on each serving plate with a spoonful of soya yogurt. Sprinkle poppy seeds (if using) and lemon zest on the yogurt to decorate and serve.

Serves 4

Opposite: Fruit crepes

VEGAN

LUXURY MUESLI

Many of the ready-made muesli mixes contain not only sugar but also dried milk powder – a product you may wish to avoid if you're following a low-fat, dairy-free or vegan diet.

225 g/8 oz wheat flakes

225 g/8 oz rolled oat flakes (porridge oats)

225 g/8 oz barley flakes

75 g/3 oz each of raw or lightly toasted hazelnuts, almonds, brazil nuts and pecans

75 g/3 oz dates, chopped

75 g/3 oz each of dried figs, apricots, peaches and pears, chopped

175 g/6 oz sultanas

75 g/3 oz raisins

50 g/2 oz dried banana flakes

■ Mix all the muesli ingredients together and store in an airtight container. Serve with milk or soya milk and fresh fruit (e.g. grapes and strawberries).

Makes 30 x 65 g/2½ oz servings

PER SERVING
■

108 kcals (458 kj)

Protein 4.5 g

Carbohydrate 30 g

Fat 0.4 g

Fibre 3 g

NOTE
■

Muesli is even better if it is pre-soaked. Put the muesli in a serving dish, allowing about 65 g/ 2½ oz per person. Pour over the milk or soya milk to taste and stir well. Leave in the refrigerator, covered, overnight. Add extra milk and fruit to serve. (If you are really cutting down on fat, soak the muesli overnight in a mixture of half water, half milk instead.)

GRILLED HONEYED
CITRUS FRUITS WITH YOGURT

This is a good winter breakfast, high in Vitamin C. By grilling the fruits quickly they are more tempting on a cold day.

1 pink/ruby grapefruit

1 yellow grapefruit

2 large oranges

2 tablespoons liquid honey

pinch of ground cinnamon, cloves and nutmeg

150 ml/5 fl oz low-fat natural yogurt

citrus fruit zest, blanched, to decorate

■ Peel and segment all the citrus fruit and place in a shallow heatproof dish.
■ In a small bowl, mix the honey and ground spices together and then drizzle over the fruit.
■ Preheat the grill to high and place the dish under the grill for 5 minutes, lowering the heat to medium after 1 minute.
■ Serve with natural yogurt, decorated with citrus fruit zest.

Serves 4

PER SERVING
■

122 kcals (513 kj)

Protein 4 g

Fat 0.6 g

Carbohydrate 30 g

Added sugar 10 g

Fibre 3 g

BAKED APPLE
WITH SAVOURY FILLING

Baked apples are usually served with sweet fillings, but the tartness of the apple makes a delicious contrast with the savoury ingredients in this recipe – the sort of ingredients that are often used for a vegetarian sausage mixture.

PER SERVING
■
128 kcals (541 kj)
Protein 2 g
Fat 3 g
Carbohydrate 25 g
Fibre 4.5 g

2 teaspoons groundnut oil
1 small onion, very finely chopped
50 g/2 oz mushrooms, very finely chopped
15 g/½ oz walnuts, very finely chopped
15 g/½ oz wholemeal breadcrumbs
2 teaspoons chopped parsley
1 teaspoon chopped sage
salt and freshly ground black pepper
4 Bramley cooking apples

■ Preheat the oven to 190°C/375°F/Gas Mark 5.
■ Heat the oil in a small saucepan and gently cook the onion, mushrooms and walnuts together for about 5 minutes until soft. Remove from the heat and stir in the breadcrumbs, herbs and seasoning to taste.
■ Remove the cores from the apples, then run a sharp knife round the skin in a spiral from top to bottom. Fill the centre of each apple and place on a greased baking sheet.
■ Bake in the preheated oven for 25–30 minutes until the apples are tender when tested with the point of a sharp knife.

Serves 4

BAKED BEANS IN
TOMATO SAUCE

PER SERVING
■

140 kcals (585 kj)
Protein 6 g
Fat 0.6 g
Carbohydrate 30 g
Fibre 5 g

If you are using molasses as a sweetener as in this recipe, try to get unsulphured blackstrap molasses which contain calcium and iron, sometimes in quite significant amounts if iron vats have been used for storage. These baked beans are best made in advance and reheated for breakfast as they take quite a long time to cook.

450 g/1 lb dried haricot beans, soaked overnight in cold water
90 ml/3 fl oz blackstrap molasses
25 g/1 oz dark muscovado sugar
1 teaspoon mustard powder
1 small onion, finely chopped
150 ml/¼ pint passata
2 tablespoons tomato purée
salt and pepper
wholemeal toast, to serve

■ Preheat the oven to 180°C/350°F/Gas Mark 4.
■ Drain the beans and place in a pan of cold water. Bring to the boil. Boil for 10 minutes, then reduce to a simmer and cook until the beans are tender (about 30 minutes). Drain the beans, reserving the liquid, and place in a casserole dish.
■ In a bowl, mix the molasses with 300 ml/½ pint of the reserved liquid. Add the sugar, mustard powder, onion, passata and tomato purée and pour the mixture over the beans.
■ Cover the casserole and cook in the preheated oven for about an hour until the sauce has thickened. Season to taste and serve with wholemeal toast.

Serves 6

SCRAMBLED TOFU

The addition of the fresh vegetables not only adds flavour to this dish but also makes it quite a good source of Vitamin C.

300 g/10 oz firm tofu
1 tablespoon vegetable oil
1 small onion, finely chopped
½ red pepper, deseeded and finely diced
1 stick celery, finely diced
50 g/2 oz mushrooms, finely diced
½ teaspoon turmeric
½–1 tablespoon shoyu
freshly ground black pepper

■ Drain the tofu and mash with a fork. Heat the oil in a frying pan and sauté all the vegetables until soft. Add the mashed tofu and turmeric and mix well.

■ Cook for a further 2 minutes, stirring all the time. Season to taste with shoyu and black pepper and serve hot with toast.

Serves 3–4

PER SERVING

■

92 kcals (381 kj)
Protein 6 g
Fat 6 g
Carbohydrate 4 g
Fibre 0.8 g

TOFU KEDGEREE

Kedgeree is often served for breakfast or a light supper. It needs lots of seasoning because the rice absorbs the flavours.

175 g/6 oz long-grain rice
50 g/2 oz butter
225 g/8 oz smoked tofu, drained and cut into 1-cm/½-in cubes
pinch of cayenne pepper
2 free-range eggs, hard-boiled
salt and freshly ground black pepper
2 tablespoons tamari
4 tablespoons finely chopped parsley
buttered toast, to serve

■ Cook the rice in slightly salted boiling water until just tender, or according to the packet instructions. Drain and keep warm.

■ Meanwhile, melt the butter in a frying pan and sauté the tofu with a good pinch of cayenne pepper for about 5 minutes, until the tofu starts to colour.

■ Chop the hard-boiled eggs quite finely and add to the pan together with the cooked rice. Heat through thoroughly over a low heat.

■ Season with the salt, pepper and tamari and stir in half of the parsley. Turn into a serving dish and scatter the remaining parsley over the top. Serve with hot buttered toast.

Serves 4

PER SERVING

■

270 kcals (1128 kj)
Protein 13.5 g
Fat 18 g
Carbohydrate 15 g
Fibre 0.8 g

VEGAN

HEALTHY HASH
BROWNS WITH TOMATOES AND RASHERS

PER SERVING
■

188 kcals (790 kj)
Protein 10.5 g
Fat 7 g
Carbohydrate 21.5 g
Fibre 2 g

Hash browns are usually fried and tend to soak up a lot of oil. This healthier version is baked in the oven and tastes just as good.

450 g/1 lb potatoes, peeled and left whole
1 small onion, grated
1 tablespoon chopped parsley (optional)
1 tablespoon snipped chives (optional)
salt and freshly ground black pepper
1 tablespoon sunflower oil
4 beef tomatoes
1 packet smoked or marinated tofu, cut into 8 thin slices
extra oil, for brushing
sprigs of parsley and snipped chives, to garnish

■ Preheat the oven to 190°C/375°F/Gas Mark 5. Grease 2 baking sheets.
■ Parboil the potatoes in a pan of lightly salted water for about 10 minutes. Drain and leave to cool. Grate coarsely and mix in the onion and herbs (if using), and season well with salt and pepper. Add the sunflower oil and mix to bind.
■ Shape the mixture into 12 patties and place on one of the greased baking sheets. Brush with a little extra oil and bake in the preheated oven for about 20 minutes until golden and tender.
■ At the same time, brush the slices of tofu with a little oil and place on the other greased baking sheet. Cut the tomatoes in half and place on the same baking sheet. Bake in the oven for 25 minutes.
■ Serve immediately, garnished with parsley and snipped chives.

Serves 4

Opposite: Healthy hash browns with tomatoes and rashers

*CAN BE VEGAN

CREAMED
MUSHROOMS ON TOAST

A delicious breakfast treat at the weekend when you have more time to cook. You can also serve the mushrooms as a good lunchtime snack.

PER SERVING
■

357 kcals (1494 kj)
Protein 11 g
Fat 20.5 g
Carbohydrate 34 g
Fibre 5 g

15 g/½ oz butter or vegan margarine*

450 g/1 lb mushrooms, sliced

300 ml/½ pint soured cream or soya cream*

salt and freshly ground black pepper

8 slices wholemeal toast

1 teaspoon paprika

1 tablespoon chopped parsley

■ Melt the butter or vegan margarine* in a saucepan and fry the mushrooms until tender (about 10 minutes). Stir in the cream or soya cream* and season to taste with salt and pepper.

■ Cut the pieces of toast into triangles and arrange on 4 serving plates. Spoon the mushrooms over the top, sprinkle with paprika and parsley and serve.

Serves 4

FIELD MUSHROOMS
STUFFED WITH HERBY SCRAMBLED EGGS

Here's a useful tip for healthy breakfasts when you're serving eggs – if you use a good non-stick pan, you can scramble or 'fry' the eggs without using any fat.

4 very large field mushrooms
4 teaspoons groundnut oil
4 cherry tomatoes, halved
6 large free-range eggs
2 tablespoons finely chopped fresh herbs, e.g. chives, parsley and marjoram
sea salt and freshly ground black pepper

To serve:
6 slices wholemeal toast, cut into triangles
sprigs of parsley and chive flowers

■ Brush both sides of each mushroom with a little oil. Cook gently on both sides under a preheated hot grill until tender and juicy. Grill the cherry tomato halves, cut-side down, until the skin starts to char.
■ Beat the eggs together with the herbs and season to taste with salt and pepper.
■ Heat a heavy-based non-stick pan, and when hot pour in the eggs. Leave them to set for 1 minute, then stir with a wooden spoon, gently but constantly, over a medium heat until the required degree of creaminess is reached. Remove from the heat.
■ Place one mushroom on each warm serving plate. Fill with scrambled eggs. Arrange 3 triangles of toast on each plate, together with 2 grilled cherry tomato halves and a sprig of parsley and some chive flowers. Serve immediately.

Serves 4

PER SERVING
■
239 kcals (1001 kj)
Protein 15 g
Fat 14.5 g
Carbohydrates 14.5 g
Fibre 3 g

HERB BREAD

VEGAN

A delicious bread for weekend guests. Bake it the day before and serve as suggested below.

225 g/8 oz spelt flour
225 g/8 oz strong white flour
good pinch of sea salt
1 teaspoon fennel seed, lightly crushed
1 tablespoon chopped sage
1 tablespoon chopped thyme
15 g/½ oz fresh yeast (or 2 teaspoons dried yeast)
2 teaspoons soft brown sugar
300 ml/½ pint hand-hot water
extra flour, for kneading

- Preheat the oven to 230°C/450°F/Gas Mark 8. Thoroughly grease a 900-g/2-lb loaf tin or a baking sheet.
- Sift the flours into a large mixing bowl and add the salt and all the herbs.
- In a small bowl, cream the fresh yeast with the sugar and add a little of the hand-hot water. Leave in a warm place for about 10 minutes until it starts to froth. (If using dried yeast, add the water first).
- Add the yeast to the flour and herb mixture together with enough of the hand-hot water to make a soft but not sticky dough which comes away from the bowl easily.
- Turn the dough out onto a lightly floured work surface and knead for 10 minutes. Return the dough to a lightly greased bowl, cover loosely with clingfilm and leave to rise until doubled in size (45–60 minutes).
- Knock the dough back, knead again for 5 minutes, then shape and place in the prepared loaf tin, or shape into a round loaf and place on the baking sheet. Leave to prove for about 20–30 minutes.
- Bake in the preheated oven for 30–40 minutes. Turn out and cool slightly on a wire cooling rack and serve warm with butter or vegan margarine.

Serves 4

PER SERVING
■

390 kcals (1658 kj)
Protein 14.5 g
Fat 2.5 g
Carbohydrate 82.5 g
Fibre 7 g

SERVING SUGGESTION
■

Toast day-old bread, spread with a little mustard if liked, and serve topped with softly scrambled eggs or grilled tomatoes and mushrooms.

SEED BREAD

When making bread, try adding the water a tablespoon at a time and mix in well. The dough should be soft, but not sticky, and should come away from the bowl, your hands and the worktop without a trace!

PER SERVING
■

113 kcals (477 kj)
Protein 4 g
Fat 3 g
Carbohydrate 19 g
Fibre 2 g

175 g/6 oz strong wholemeal flour

175 g/6 oz strong white flour

good pinch of sea salt

15 g/½ oz fresh yeast (or 2 teaspoons dried yeast)

2 teaspoons sugar

2 teaspoons sunflower oil

300 ml/½ pint (approximately) hand-hot water

1 tablespoon each of sunflower seeds, pumpkin seeds, sesame seeds and
    poppy seeds plus extra for decoration

dairy or soya milk*, to glaze

■ Preheat the oven to 220°C/425°F/Gas Mark 7. Grease a baking sheet.

■ Make the bread, following steps 3-6 of the Cinnamon and Raisin Bread method (see page 28). Then carry on as below.

■ Knock back the dough and add the seeds, kneading them into the dough for about 5 minutes to distribute them evenly.

■ Divide the dough into 6–8 equal pieces and roll each one into a 'sausage' shape, looping one over another to make a knot, and place on the prepared baking sheet. Leave to prove for about 30 minutes.

■ Brush with milk or soya milk* to glaze. Sprinkle some extra seeds on the top, if liked, and bake in the preheated oven for 15–20 minutes. When cooked, the rolls should sound hollow when tapped on the base. Cool on a wire cooling rack.

CINNAMON AND
RAISIN BREAD

Bread doesn't have to be wholemeal to be healthy, and this tasty breakfast bread works best with white flour.

PER SERVING

■

178 kcals (759 kj)
Protein 6 g
Fat 0.7 g
Carbohydrate 40 g
Fibre 2 g

50 g/2 oz raisins
150 ml/¼ pint freshly made tea for soaking
675 g/1½ lb strong white flour
good pinch of salt
15 g/½ oz fresh yeast (or 2 teaspoons dried yeast)
2 teaspoons sugar
1 teaspoon ground cinnamon
grated zest of 1 lemon
450 ml/¾ pint hand-hot water
milk or soya milk*, to glaze

■ Soak the raisins in the tea overnight. Drain and pat dry with kitchen paper.
■ Preheat the oven to 220°C/425°F/Gas Mark 7. Thoroughly grease a 900-g/2-lb loaf tin.
■ Sift the flour and salt into a large mixing bowl. In a small mixing bowl, cream the fresh yeast with the sugar and add a little of the warm water. Leave in a warm place for about 10 minutes until it starts to froth. (If using dried yeast, add the water first).
■ Add the yeast to the flour together with enough water to make a soft but not sticky dough that comes away form the bowl easily.
■ Turn out the dough onto a lightly floured work surface and knead for 10 minutes. Return the dough to a lightly greased bowl, cover loosely with clingfilm and leave to rise until doubled in size (45–60 minutes).
■ Knock the dough back. Mix the raisins, cinnamon and lemon zest in a small bowl, then add to the dough and knead for 5 minutes, incorporating the ingredients as you go. Shape and place in the prepared loaf tin. Leave it to prove for about 20–30 minutes.
■ Brush with milk or soya milk* to glaze and bake in the preheated oven for 35–40 minutes. The bread is cooked when tapping the bottom makes a hollow sound. Turn out onto a cooling rack to go cold before slicing.

Yields 14 slices

MUESLI BREAD

VEGAN

A classic breakfast bread, this is good plain or toasted, with butter or vegan margarine, or a little fruit preserve. It will get you off to a good start for the day.

450 g/1 lb strong wholemeal or spelt flour
good pinch of salt
175 g/6 oz muesli (use ready-made, or see page 18 for Luxury Muesli)
2 tablespoons blackstrap molasses
150 ml/¼ pint warm water
15 g/½ oz fresh yeast (or 2 teaspoons dried yeast)
300 ml/½ pint hand-hot water

PER SERVING
■
76 kcals (232 kj)
Protein 3 g
Fat 0.8 g
Carbohydrate 16 g
Fibre 1.5 g

■ Preheat the oven to 200°C/400°F/Gas Mark 6. Thoroughly grease two 900-g/2-lb loaf tins.

■ Sift the flour and salt into a large mixing bowl. Then reincorporate any bran left in the sieve. Mix in the muesli and make a well in the centre.

■ In a small bowl, mix the molasses and the warm water together, then mix in the yeast and leave in a warm place for 10 minutes until frothy.

■ Add to the flour mixture with enough of the extra hand-hot water to make a soft but not sticky dough. Turn out onto a lightly floured surface and knead briefly.

■ Divide the dough between the two prepared loaf tins, cover loosely with greased clingfilm and leave in a warm place until doubled in size (about 30 minutes).

■ Remove the clingfilm and bake in the preheated oven for about 40 minutes (until it sounds hollow when tapped). Turn out onto a cooling rack and allow to go cold before slicing.

Yields 14 slices (each loaf)

*CAN BE VEGAN

SAVOURY
BREAKFAST ROLLS

This recipe is based on a very old Sussex recipe known as 'Hikers' brunch' or Sussex Sausage Rolls. You can use other fillings to make the rolls really interesting and a surprise to bite into.

PER SERVING
■

402 kcals (1698 kj)
Protein 17 g
Fat 9 g
Carbohydrate 68 g
Fibre 6 g

175 g/6 oz strong wholemeal flour
175 g/6 oz strong white flour
pinch of salt
good pinch of mixed herbs
15 g/½ oz fresh yeast
1 teaspoon sugar
450 ml/15 fl oz (approx.) hand-hot
    water

1 tablespoon sunflower oil
extra flour, for kneading
450 g/1 lb vegetarian/vegan*
    sausages of your choice (8
    sausages), cooked and cooled

VARIATIONS
■

Try enclosing a tablespoon of garlic mushrooms in each piece of dough, or a tablespoon of Onion Marmalade (see page 103) or even some finely chopped roasted vegetables for a change.

■ Preheat the oven to 220°C/425°F/Gas Mark 7. Grease a baking sheet.
■ Sift the flours and salt into a large bowl. Add the mixed herbs. In a small mixing bowl, cream the fresh yeast with the sugar and add a little of the hand-hot water. Leave in a warm place for about 10 minutes until it starts to froth (if using dried yeast, add the water first)
■ Add the yeast to the flour together with the sunflower oil. Add enough water to make a soft but not sticky dough that comes away from the bowl easily.
■ Turn the dough out onto a floured work surface and knead for 10 minutes. Return the dough to a lightly greased bowl, cover loosely with clingfilm and leave to rise until doubled in size (45–60 minutes).
■ Knock the dough back, knead for a couple of minutes and then cut into 8 equal-sized pieces. Roll each piece out to a rectangle, a little longer than each sausage and about 7.5 cm/3 in wide, and form each piece around a cold sausage – the dough should be about 0.75–1.25 cm/¼–½ in thick all over.
■ Place on the greased baking sheet and leave to rise for about 20–30 minutes until the dough has doubled in size.
■ Bake in the preheated oven for about 15 minutes, then reduce the oven temperature to 180°C/350°F/Gas Mark 4 for a further 20 minutes. Eat warm or cold with the relish of your choice.

Yields 8 rolls

Opposite: Savoury breakfast rolls and Breakfast muffins (page 33)

SAVOURY MUFFINS
WITH SUN-DRIED TOMATOES AND HERBS

Muffins are so easy to make and the flavourings can be varied endlessly – use the basic recipe together with your imagination to generate more combinations.

175 g/6 oz plain flour (white or wholemeal)
½ tablespoon baking powder
good pinch of salt
I large free-range egg, beaten
100 ml/4 fl oz milk
50 g/2 oz butter, softened
25 g/I oz sun-dried tomatoes (dry – not in oil), finely chopped
good pinch of dried mixed Italian herbs
freshly ground black pepper
25 g/I oz vegetarian pecorino cheese, very finely grated (optional)

■ Preheat the oven to 200°C/400°F/Gas Mark 6. Line a deep muffin tin with muffin cases.
■ Reconstitute the tomatoes with boiling water, then drain and pat dry with kitchen paper.
■ Sift the flour, baking powder and salt into a large bowl. Add the egg, milk and softened butter, then use a hand whisk to beat all the ingredients together quickly.
■ Quickly fold in the tomatoes and herbs and black pepper and spoon into the muffin cases (each should be about two-thirds full). Sprinkle the top of each one with pecorino, if using.
■ Bake in the preheated oven for about 30 minutes, until well risen and golden in colour. Cool on a wire rack.

Makes 6 large muffins

PER SERVING
■

212 kcals (887 kj)
Protein 6 g
Fat 12 g
Carbohydrate 21 g
Fibre I g

SERVING SUGGESTION
■

Serve while still slightly warm with scrambled eggs into which fresh chives have been snipped.

BREAKFAST MUFFINS

Best eaten fresh, these muffins are very quick to make using the all-in-one method.

Basic mixture:
350 g/12 oz plain white flour
1 tablespoon baking powder
175 g/6 oz light muscovado sugar
150 g/50 g butter, softened (or soft margarine)
3 large free-range eggs
150 ml/¼ pint milk

Banana and date:
1 ripe banana, mashed
100 g/4 oz dates, finely chopped

Apple and cinnamon:
1 dessert apple, peeled, cored and grated
½ teaspoon ground cinnamon

PER MUFFIN (BANANA AND DATE)
■
245 kcals (1038 kj)
Protein 5.9 g
Fat 2.3 g
Carbohydrate 53.7 g
Fibre 1.8 g

■ Preheat the oven to 200°C/400°F/Gas Mark 6. Line a deep muffin tin with muffin cases.

■ Sift the flour and baking powder into a large bowl. Add the sugar and stir well.

■ Add the butter, eggs and milk and whisk together quickly. Put half of the mixture into a clean bowl.

■ Fold the banana and dates into one bowl of the mixture and the apple and cinnamon into the other.

■ Spoon the two mixtures into separate muffin cases (each case should be about two-thirds full).

■ Bake in the preheated oven until well risen and golden (about 15–20 minutes). Cool on a wire rack.

Makes 12 (6 of each flavour)

PER MUFFIN (APPLE AND CINNAMON)
■
191 kcals (804 kj)
Protein 5.2 g
Fat 2.3 g
Carbohydrate 40 g
Fibre 1.1 g

APPETISERS
AND LIGHT BITES

Left: Chinese-style lettuce wraps (page 42)

TUSCAN
TOMATO SOUP

PER SERVING

■

230 kcals (965 kj)
Protein 7 g
Fat 8 g
Carbohydrate 35 g
Fibre 3 g

This very simple rustic soup would be made in Italy with fresh tomatoes, but to improve the flavour a mixture of passata and roasted tomatoes is used here. The bread gives an unusual texture to the soup, which you can serve for a substantial lunch.

450 g/1 lb ripe, full-flavour tomatoes
4 garlic cloves, skins left on
2 tablespoons olive oil
1 onion, finely chopped
450 g/1 lb passata
1 litre/1¾ pints tomato and herb stock
  (made with stock cubes)
1 small baguette
1 small bunch of basil
salt and freshly ground black pepper

■ Preheat the oven to 200°C/400°F/Gas Mark 6.

■ Place the tomatoes and garlic in a roasting pan and drizzle with 1 tablespoon olive oil. Roast in the preheated oven for about 1 hour until the skins are blackening. Remove the garlic after 30 minutes and skin.

■ Heat the remaining oil in a large saucepan and fry the onion until soft and golden. Add the roasted tomatoes with all their juices, the garlic, passata and stock. Bring to the boil, then cover the pan and simmer for 30 minutes.

■ Remove from the heat and cool before blending the soup thoroughly in a blender or food processor, making sure that all the tomato skins are blended. Return the soup to a clean saucepan.

■ Cut the ends off the baguette and discard. Cut the baguette into small cubes and stir into the soup while reheating. Cook gently for about 10 minutes.

■ Tear the basil leaves into rough pieces and add to the soup just before serving. Season to taste with salt and pepper and serve in a tureen or individual bowls.

Serves 4

WATERCRESS SOUP

VEGAN

Watercress is full of iron and vitamin C. This soup freezes well and keeps for about two to three months, and can be reheated from frozen.

2 teaspoons sunflower oil
1 onion, finely chopped
100 g/4 oz potatoes, peeled, diced, rinsed and drained
2 bunches of watercress
900 ml/1½ pints vegetable stock
juice of 1 orange
150 ml/¼ pint soya milk
1 tablespoon shoyu or tamari
pinch of ground nutmeg
salt and freshly ground black pepper
4 teaspoons soya cream
sprigs of watercress and orange zest, to garnish

■ Heat the oil in a large saucepan. Sauté the onion and potatoes for 5 minutes.
■ Chop the watercress leaves and stalks, discarding any really woody pieces. Add to the pan with the stock and orange juice. Bring to the boil, then cover the pan and simmer gently for 15–20 minutes.
■ Remove from the heat and cool, then blend in a blender or food processor until smooth.
■ Return to the heat and add the soya milk and shoyu or tamari. Reheat gently and season to taste with nutmeg, salt and pepper.
■ Serve the soup immediately in individual bowls, topped with a swirl of soya cream and garnished with watercress sprigs and orange zest.

Serves 4

PER SERVING
■
122 kcals (509 kj)
Protein 4.5 g
Fat 5 g
Carbohydrate 9 g
Fibre 1 g

CARROT SOUP

VEGAN

PER SERVING
■
93 kcals (386 kj)
Protein 2 g
Fat 3 g
Carbohydrate 16 g
Fibre 5 g

Carrots, like many other orange and red vegetables, are high in betacarotene which the body converts to Vitamin A.

1 onion, chopped
1 garlic clove, chopped
1 tablespoon oil
675 g/1½ lb carrots, chopped
1 teaspoon grated fresh ginger root

salt and freshly ground black pepper
900 ml/1½ pints light vegetable stock
1 tablespoon chopped parsley or
    fresh coriander, to garnish

■ Sauté the onion and garlic in the oil for 5 minutes in a covered pan without browning. Add the carrots, ginger and a sprinkling of salt. Cover and lightly fry for a further 10 minutes, stirring occasionally.

■ Add the stock, bring to the boil, then reduce the heat and simmer for 15 minutes, or until the carrots are tender. Purée the soup in a blender, then return to the pan and reheat. Serve garnished with chopped fresh herbs.

Serves 4

MISO SOUP

VEGAN

PER SERVING
■
95 kcals (399 kj)
Protein 5 g
Fat 3 g
Carbohydrate 12 g
Fibre 1 g

Miso is a savoury paste made from fermented soya beans and is used to flavour soups, stews, pâtés, etc. Use sparingly.

1 teaspoon groundnut oil
2 onions, thinly sliced
2 garlic cloves, crushed
2.5-cm/1-inch piece fresh root
    ginger, peeled and grated
900 ml/1½ pints vegetable stock

100g/4 oz mooli (daikon/white
    radish)
15 g/½ oz aramé, soaked for 10
    minutes
3 tablespoons barley miso
2 spring onions, shredded, to garnish

■ Heat the oil and sauté the onions and garlic for about 5 minutes. Add the ginger, vegetable stock, mooli and aramé. Bring to the boil, then reduce the heat and simmer gently for 15–20 minutes.

■ Put the miso into a small bowl and cream it with a little of the hot soup. Pour into the saucepan and stir well. Serve garnished with spring onions.

Serves 4

Opposite: Carrot soup and Miso soup

PUMPKIN
AND HARICOT BEAN SOUP

Pumpkins are harvested in the autumn and are often hollowed out and carved into a wicked face lantern for Hallowe'en. However, pumpkin is delicious to eat and there are many different varieties to choose from. Pumpkin has a high water content so you may lose some of the bulk when you cook it. This nutritious soup is excellent for serving at a Hallowe'en party as you can use the flesh for making the soup, then carve the shell into a lantern. If you can't buy a pumpkin, use butternut squash instead.

PER SERVING

227 kcals (948 kj)
Protein: 8 g
Fat: 4.5 g
Carbohydrate: 41 g
Fibre: 9 g

1 tablespoon olive oil
1 large onion, finely chopped
2 garlic cloves, crushed
675 g/1½ lb pumpkin flesh, cubed
450 g/1 lb sweet potatoes, peeled and cubed
1 teaspoon mixed dried herbs
1 teaspoon chopped sage
1.5 litres/2½ pints vegetable stock
400-g/14-oz can of haricot beans, rinsed and drained
salt and freshly ground black pepper

■ Heat the oil in a large saucepan and gently fry the onion and garlic for about 10 minutes until softened and starting to colour. Add the pumpkin, sweet potato and herbs and cook gently for 5 minutes.
■ Add the vegetable stock and bring to the boil. Cover the pan and simmer for 30 minutes until the vegetables are cooked and tender.
■ Add the haricot beans and season to taste with salt and pepper. Cook for 5 minutes, then serve hot with crusty bread.

Serves 4

CHICK PEA
AND SPINACH SOUP

Chick peas are high in protein and phosphorus, sulphur and potassium. They are one of the most popular and tasty pulses and can even be sprouted to increase their nutritional value.

2 teaspoons sunflower oil
1 onion, finely chopped
1 garlic clove, crushed
1 teaspoon cumin seeds, lightly crushed
100 g/4 oz potato, diced and rinsed under running cold water
900 ml/1½ pints vegetable stock
400 g/14 oz can chick peas, rinsed, drained and roughly chopped
100 g/4 oz finely chopped spinach
2 tablespoons shoyu
salt and freshly ground black pepper

■ Heat the oil in a large saucepan. Sauté the onion, garlic and cumin seeds together for 5 minutes until starting to soften.

■ Drain the potatoes and add to the onions. Continue to cook for 5 minutes, stirring occasionally. Add the stock and bring to the boil. Cover the pan, reduce the heat and simmer for 15–20 minutes until the potatoes are cooked. Add the spinach and cook for 2 minutes.

■ Remove from the heat, add half of the chick peas and blend the soup in a food processor, using the pulse button to thicken the soup, until smooth.

■ Return to the pan, add the remaining chick peas, shoyu and seasoning to taste. Reheat thoroughly for 5–10 minutes and serve immediately with fresh crusty bread.

Serves 4

PER SERVING
■
177 kcals (745 kj)
Protein 10 g
Fat 5.5 g
Carbohydrate 24 g
Fibre 5 g

CHINESE-STYLE
LETTUCE WRAPS

An interesting dish to serve as a starter for an oriental meal, these wraps will be a talking point. Tofu is an excellent vegetarian source of protein.

PER SERVING

■

113 kcals (471 kj)
Protein 4 g
Fat 5 g
Carbohydrate 12 g
Added sugar 5 g
Fibre 0.5 g

100 g/4 oz firm tofu
2 tablespoons shoyu
1 garlic clove, crushed
2.5-cm/1-inch piece fresh root
    ginger, peeled and grated
1 tablespoon liquid honey
15 g/½ oz dried shiitake mushrooms
1 tablespoon groundnut oil
1 small onion, very finely chopped
50 g/2 oz water chestnuts, finely
    shredded
50 g/2 oz bamboo shoots, finely
    shredded

salt, to taste
1 teaspoon sesame oil
8 large iceberg lettuce leaves

For the dipping sauce:
50 ml/2 fl oz shoyu
1 tablespoon mirin (or vegetarian
    sherry)
2.5-cm/1-inch piece fresh root
    ginger, peeled, grated and
    squeezed
few drops of tabasco sauce
1 teaspoon sesame oil

■ Finely chop the tofu (to resemble mince). Mix the shoyu, garlic, ginger, and honey together and marinate the tofu in this mixture for 30 minutes or longer.
■ Cover the dried shiitake mushrooms with boiling water and leave to soak for 20 minutes. Discard the stalks and chop the mushrooms finely.
■ For the dipping sauce, mix all the ingredients together and place in a small bowl.
■ Heat the groundnut oil in a frying pan and fry the onion for 2 minutes. Add the marinated tofu together with any remaining marinade, the mushrooms, water chestnuts, bamboo shoots and salt to taste. Fry gently for about 3 minutes. Stir in the sesame oil.
■ Place 1–2 tablespoons of the mixture in the centre of each lettuce leaf. Fold in the sides and roll into a neat parcel (secure with a cocktail stick if necessary). Serve immediately with the dipping sauce.

Serves 4

Opposite: Chinese-style lettuce wraps

VEGAN

BROAD BEAN,
LEMON AND SAGE DIP

PER SERVING

■

97 kcals (403 kj)
Protein 7 g
Fat 6 g
Carbohydrate 4 g
Fibre 2 g

Broad beans are in season from the end of May through to the end of July, but as the season progresses they tend to become tougher. If you are using fresh broad beans, you need 100 g/4 oz of shelled beans for this recipe. Frozen broad beans are also good and almost as nutritious as freshly picked beans. The combination of flavours in this dip has a really fresh taste. Make it a little thicker and use it as a sandwich filling with crisp lettuce leaves or rocket.

1 tablespoon sunflower oil
1 small onion, finely chopped
225 g/8 oz silken tofu
1 garlic clove, crushed
zest and juice of 1 lemon
5 tablespoons soya milk
1 tablespoon shoyu
1 tablespoon chopped sage leaves
100 g/4 oz broad beans, cooked
salt and freshly ground black pepper

■ Heat the oil and gently fry the onion until softened. Cool.
■ Drain the silken tofu and place in a blender. Add the crushed garlic, lemon juice and half of the lemon zest together with the soya milk, shoyu, sage and broad beans. Blend to a smooth dipping consistency.
■ Season to taste and serve in a bowl, garnished with the reserved lemon zest, with raw vegetable crudités and pitta bread fingers.

Serves 4

MINTY PEA DIP

Frozen peas are a good source of vitamin C. This dip is a vivid bright green in colour, so there is no mistaking the main ingredient!

225 g/8 oz frozen peas
15 g/½ oz chives, snipped
15 g/½ oz mint leaves, chopped
½ green chilli, deseeded and finely chopped

grated zest and juice of ½ lemon
pinch of salt
extra lemon zest and mint leaves, to garnish
vegetable crudités, to serve

■ Place the peas in a sieve and pour boiling water over to thaw them.
■ Blend all the ingredients to a smooth purée. (If necessary, add a little water to thin the mixture.) Season to taste and transfer to a serving dish.
■ Cover and set aside at room temperature for 30 minutes before serving, to allow the flavours to develop. Serve, garnished with lemon zest and herbs, with a selection of vegetable crudités.

Serves 4

PER SERVING
■
40 kcals (171 kj)
Protein 4 g
Fat 0.6 g
Carbohydrate 6 g
Fibre 3 g

ITALIAN PATE

Ricotta and cottage cheese are both low in fat and add flavour and texture. For a dairy-free version use silken tofu*.

225 g/8 oz ricotta (or cottage cheese or silken tofu*)
½ red onion, finely chopped
1 tablespoon finely chopped olives
2 ripe tomatoes, skinned, deseeded and finely chopped

1–2 tablespoons finely chopped basil
1 teaspoon vegan horseradish sauce (or mustard)
salt and pepper
few sprigs of basil, to garnish

■ Drain the ricotta (or cottage cheese or silken tofu*, if using) and push through a sieve. In a large bowl, mix together all the ingredients, stirring gently. Cover the bowl with clingfilm and chill slightly before serving.
■ Serve the pâté in a small bowl, or place individual servings on each plate garnished with fresh herbs.

Serves 4

PER SERVING
■
70 kcals (298 kj)
Protein 8 g
Fat 2 g
Carbohydrate 6 g
Fibre 1 g

*CAN BE VEGAN

FATTOUSH WITH
LAMB'S LETTUCE

PER SERVING

■

141 kcals (589 kj)
Protein 7 g
Fat 10 g
Carbohydrate 7 g
Fibre 2 g

This substantial salad is suitable for serving as a light meal. If you want to avoid using the cheese and egg, try substituting finely chopped, grilled smoked or marinated tofu.

½ cos lettuce, washed and shredded
50 g/2 oz lamb's lettuce, washed
4 ripe tomatoes, each cut into
    8 wedges
¼ cucumber, diced
5 spring onions, finely sliced
12 kalamata olives, stoned
15 g/½ oz mint, chopped
15 g/½ oz parsley, chopped
75 g/3 oz feta cheese, diced (omit
    for vegan*)
2 free-range eggs, hard-boiled (omit
    for vegan*)

For the dressing:

juice of 1 lemon
2 tablespoons olive oil
1 teaspoon wholegrain mustard
1 teaspoon chopped mint
1 teaspoon chopped parsley
1 garlic clove, crushed
salt and freshly ground black pepper

For the croûtons:

2 slices white bread, toasted and
    crusts removed
1 garlic clove, peeled

■ Make the dressing by whisking all the ingredients together until thoroughly blended.

■ Mix the lettuces, tomatoes, cucumber, spring onions, olives, mint and parsley together in a bowl. Pour over the dressing and toss well. Turn into a salad bowl.

■ If using the feta cheese, scatter over the salad and mix in. If using the hard-boiled eggs, shell and chop finely and sprinkle over the salad.

■ Rub the whole garlic clove over the surface of each piece of toast. Cut the toast into bite-sized croûtons and scatter over the salad. Serve immediately.

Serves 6

Opposite: Fattoush with lamb's lettuce

VEGAN

MALAYSIAN
VERMICELLI

PER SERVING

■

213 kcals (889 kj)
Protein 11 g
Fat 8.5 g
Carbohydrate 27 g
Fibre 2 g

Marinated tofu pieces are extremely useful for stir-fries or stews. You can buy packs of these tofu chunks in health food stores or supermarkets. They have been partly cooked so that they keep their shape and texture well when added to a dish.

2.5-cm/1-inch piece of cinnamon stick
4 green cardamoms
1 teaspoon coriander seeds
1 teaspoon cumin seeds
6 whole cloves
1 tablespoon groundnut oil
1 large onion, finely chopped
2 garlic cloves, crushed
½ teaspoon chilli powder
400-g/14-oz can of chopped tomatoes, drained

2.5-cm/1-inch piece fresh root ginger, peeled, grated and juice squeezed out
juice of 1 lemon
225 g/8 oz marinated tofu pieces, roughly chopped
150 ml/¼ pint water
salt, to taste
200 g/7 oz beansprouts
75 g/3 oz rice vermicelli, cooked
25 g/1 oz roasted peanuts, chopped

■ Heat a dry non-stick frying pan and add all the whole spices. Toss in the pan until they release their aromas, and then grind to a fine powder.

■ Heat the groundnut oil in a wok and cook the onion and garlic for about 5 minutes until lightly browned. Add the ground spices and chilli powder and cook for 2 minutes. Add the tomatoes and cook for 5 more minutes to a chunky paste.

■ Add the ginger, lemon juice, tofu and water and bring to the boil, stirring. Reduce the heat and simmer gently for about 5–10 minutes until the sauce thickens.

■ Season to taste with salt and pepper, add the beansprouts and cook for 2 minutes. Add the vermicelli and toss well to coat in the tofu sauce. Scatter the chopped roasted peanuts over the top and serve immediately.

Serves 4

BURMESE-STYLE
STIR-FRY

VEGAN

There are lots of fresh vegetables in this dish and as they are cooked quickly by stir-frying, the vitamin content remains high. Although the fat content is quite high, you drain the fried tofu on kitchen paper to remove any excess.

250 g/9 oz firm regular tofu
4 tablespoons groundnut oil

Stir-fry:
375 g/12 oz egg-free noodles
1 teaspoon groundnut oil
2 shallots, sliced
4 garlic cloves, finely chopped
1 red chilli, finely chopped
50 g/2 oz bamboo shoots, shredded
50 g/2 oz water chestnuts, sliced
50 g/2 oz baby sweetcorn, halved lengthways
100 g/4 oz Chinese leaves, shredded
100 g/4 oz baby spinach leaves, shredded
100 g/4 oz beansprouts
2 tablespoons shoyu
1 teaspoon sesame oil

■ Drain and press the tofu to remove excess liquid. Cut into cubes and then into triangles. Heat the oil in a non-stick frying pan and fry the tofu until golden on both sides. Drain well on kitchen paper and keep warm.

■ Cook the noodles, according to the packet instructions, for about 4 minutes. Drain and keep warm.

■ In a wok, heat the groundnut oil. When very hot, add the shallots, garlic and chilli and cook, stirring all the time, until golden. Add the bamboo shoots, water chestnuts and sweetcorn and cook for 2 minutes.

■ Add the shredded Chinese leaves and spinach and stir-fry for 2–3 minutes until the spinach has wilted. Add the beansprouts and reserved tofu and mix well. Stir in the shoyu and sesame oil and serve on a bed of noodles.

Serves 4

PER SERVING
■
260 kcals (1081 kj)
Protein 10 g
Fat 16 g
Carbohydrate 19 g
Fibre 2 g

POTATO PIZZA WITH
MIXED PEPPER AND MUSHROOM TOPPING

PER SERVING
■
259 kcals (1089 kj)
Protein 7 g
Fat 9 g
Carbohydrate 39 g
Fibre 5 g

The potatoes make a much lighter base than a traditional bread pizza, and the colourful pepper and mushroom topping is a good source of vitamins.

225 g/8 oz potatoes, chopped
25 g/1 oz butter or vegan margarine*
salt and pepper
100 g/4 oz self-raising flour (white)
2 tablespoons tomato purée
1 tablespoon olive oil
1 large onion, sliced
1 red pepper, deseeded and sliced

1 orange or yellow pepper, deseeded and sliced
1 green pepper, deseeded and sliced
100 g/4 oz mushrooms, sliced
1 teaspoon dried oregano
1 tablespoon cider vinegar
225 g/8 oz spinach leaves
2 tablespoons vegetarian Parmesan cheese (optional)

■ Preheat the oven to 200°C/400°F/Gas Mark 6.
■ Boil the potatoes in a large pan of salted water until tender. Drain well and mash with the butter or margarine* until smooth. Season with salt and pepper.
■ While still warm, stir in the flour, and then turn out onto a lightly floured worktop and knead for 2 minutes. Press into a round on a greased baking sheet, using your fingers, and spread the tomato purée evenly over the surface.
■ Heat the olive oil in a frying pan. Fry the onion and peppers for 5 minutes until starting to soften, then add the mushrooms and cook for a further 5 minutes until tender. Stir in the dried oregano, cider vinegar and seasoning. Remove from the heat.
■ Wash the spinach leaves thoroughly and cook gently in a covered pan for 2 minutes in the water remaining on the leaves until bright green and wilted. Drain well.
■ Spread the spinach leaves evenly over the pizza base, followed by the onion mixture. Sprinkle with Parmesan, if using, and bake in the preheated oven for 20–30 minutes until the edges of the base look golden and crispy. Serve immediately with a green salad.

Serves 4

Opposite: Potato pizza with mixed pepper and mushroom topping

VEGAN

ROAST PEPPER
AND AUBERGINE MOUSSE

PER SERVING
■
65 kcals (271 kj)
Protein 4.5 g
Fat 3 g
Carbohydrate 5 g
Fibre 3 g

High in beta-carotene, the red peppers also give this mousse a distinctive colour. This dish makes a delicious light lunch or a good dinner party starter.

1 aubergine	1 garlic clove, crushed
1 teaspoon groundnut oil	salt and freshly ground black pepper
2 large red peppers	2½ tablespoons agar agar flakes
juice of 1 lemon	125 ml/5 fl oz water
225 g/8 oz silken tofu	sprigs of parsley, to garnish
150 ml/¼ pint soya milk	melba toasts, to serve

■ Preheat the oven to 180°C/350°F/ Gas Mark 4.

■ Brush the aubergine with the oil, place on a baking sheet with the red peppers and bake in the preheated oven for 45 minutes.

■ Allow to cool a little, then peel the aubergine, and skin and deseed the peppers, reserving the juices. Chop the flesh, reserving a few strips of red pepper for the garnish.

■ Put the flesh and reserved juices in a blender or food processor with the lemon juice, tofu, soya milk, crushed garlic and seasoning. Blend until smooth.

■ Put the agar agar and water in a saucepan. Heat gently at first, then bring to the boil, stirring all the time. Simmer for 5–10 minutes until completely dissolved.

■ Stir the agar agar into the pepper and aubergine mixture and blend again. Pour immediately into individual ramekin dishes, tapping each one sharply on the worktop to remove any air bubbles. Refrigerate for at least 30 minutes to set.

■ Decorate with the reserved red pepper strips and serve garnished with parsley sprigs with the melba toasts.

Serves 6

CAPONATA CROSTINI

VEGAN

Traditional crostini bases are brushed with oil before baking in the oven, but you can make a low-fat version quite simply by omiting the oil and baking the bread dry – it won't be as golden, but it will still be crisp.

1 baguette, cut into 1.25-cm/½-inch thick slices

2 large garlic cloves, left whole

3 plum tomatoes, skinned and roughly chopped

1 small red onion, finely sliced

100 g/4 oz stoned green olives, roughly chopped

1½ tablespoons capers

25 g/1 oz pine kernels

salt and freshly ground pepper

flat-leaf parsley, to garnish

- Preheat the oven to 200°C/400°F/Gas Mark 6.
- Place the bread slices on a baking sheet and bake in the preheated oven until golden – rub with the whole cloves of garlic.
- Mix the tomatoes, onion, olives, capers and pine kernels together and season well. Pile the mixture on top of the crostini bases and garnish with flat-leaf parsley.

Serves 6

PER SERVING
■
282 kcals (1194 kj)
Protein 9 g
Fat 7 g
Carbohydrate 48 g
Fibre 2 g

ROAST VEGETABLE
TORTILLAS WITH FROMAGE FRAIS AND MINT DRESSING

PER SERVING
■

407 kcals (1711 kj)
Protein 15 g
Fat 12 g
Carbohydrate 64 g
Fibre 7 g

Fromage frais contains between one and eight per cent fat, so it is ideal for low-fat dressings. Check the label to make sure that it is suitable for vegetarians as it may be thickened with animal rennet.

2 tablespoons olive oil
salt and freshly ground black pepper
1 garlic clove, crushed
1 aubergine, cubed
3 courgettes, cubed
1 red pepper, deseeded and cubed
1 yellow pepper, deseeded and
    cubed
8 shallots, halved
12 garlic cloves, peeled and left
    whole
1 bulb fennel, diced
100 g/4 oz cherry tomatoes, halved

25 g/1 oz pine nuts, toasted
few drops of Tabasco
8 large soft flour tortillas
sprigs of mint, to garnish

**Fromage frais
and mint dressing:**
200 g/7 oz very low fat natural
    fromage frais
15 g/½ oz fresh mint
2 teaspoons white wine vinegar
1 teaspoon apple juice concentrate

■ Preheat the oven to 200°C/400°F/Gas Mark 6.

■ Mix the olive oil, salt and pepper and crushed garlic together.

■ Put all the vegetables, except the cherry tomatoes, in a roasting pan. Pour over the olive oil mixture and toss well to coat. Roast in the preheated oven for 25 minutes.

■ Stir the vegetables around and add the cherry tomatoes and roast for a further 5–10 minutes until the vegetables are cooked and starting to char a little.

■ Remove from the oven and stir in the pine nuts and a few drops of tabasco. At the same time, wrap the tortillas in foil and warm through in the oven for 10 minutes.

■ Meanwhile, make the dressing by beating all the ingredients together.

■ Divide the roast vegetable mixture equally between the warm tortillas. Roll up and serve immediately with the dressing drizzled over them, garnished with sprigs of mint.

Serves 4

SAVOURY FILO
TRIANGLES

These filo triangles are delicious made with tofu, but if you prefer dairy foods, substitute ricotta or cottage cheese.

225 g/8 oz filo pastry
2 tablespoons olive oil

Tofu and spinach filling:
1 small onion, finely chopped
1 tablespoon olive oil
50 g/2 oz crumbled tofu*/ricotta cheese
1 tablespoon tahini
25 g/1 oz stoned olives, chopped
150 g/5 oz spinach, blanched, drained and chopped (if frozen, thawed, drained and chopped)
25 g/1 oz breadcrumbs
pinch of freshly grated nutmeg
15 g/½ oz basil leaves, chopped
salt and pepper

■ Preheat the oven to 190°C/375°F/Gas Mark 5.
■ To make the filling, sauté the onion gently in the oil until soft and golden.
■ In a bowl, cream the tofu* or ricotta with the tahini until smooth. Mix in all the remaining ingredients, including the onion, and season to taste with salt and pepper.
■ Cut the filo sheets into 8-cm/3-inch × 30-cm/12-inch strips. Use 2 strips at a time, keeping the rest covered. Brush one strip lightly with olive oil, then place the second strip on top and brush lightly again.
■ Place 1 tablespoon of the filling mixture on one end of the strip. Fold the corner of the pastry over the filling to make a triangle and continue folding up the length of the strip, maintaining a triangular shape as you go. Repeat the filling and folding process with all the filo strips.
■ Place on an oiled baking sheet (with sides) and bake in the preheated oven for about 20 minutes until crisp and golden.

Serves 6

PER SERVING
■
191 kcals (795 kj)
Protein 5 g
Fat 8.5 g
Carbohydrate 25 g
Added sugar 0.9 g
Fibre 1 g

MAIN-
COURSE DISHES

Bubble and squeak patties
Farfalle with mange tout, flageolet beans,
   courgettes and mint
Penne with broccoli, avocado and roast pepper
Asparagus fettucine stir-fry with peanut sauce
Millet pilaf
Wild mushroom risotto
Vegetable and black eye bean bangalore
Mushroom, pepper and tomato stew with
   quinoa
Nutty flan with tofu and vegetable filling
Sweet and sour cabbage parcels
Enchiladas with warm tomato salsa
Szechuan tofu
Marinated tofu and vegetable filo pie
Broad bean and sweetcorn stew
Patatas bravas
Spiced red cabbage
Quick-fried shredded kohlrabi
Sweet baked beetroot
Celeriac mash
Teriyaki stir-fry

Left: Nutty flan with tofu and vegetable filling (page 68)

*CAN BE VEGAN

BUBBLE AND SQUEAK
PATTIES

This combination makes an interesting vegetarian 'burger'. Serve in a burger bun with salad, or with other vegetables. Although this dish is included as a main meal, you could omit the garlic and serve the burgers with tomatoes and vegetarian rashers for an interesting breakfast.

450 g/1 lb potatoes, cooked and mashed
225 g/8 oz cabbage, finely shredded and cooked
15 g/½ oz butter or vegan margarine*
salt and pepper
1 tablespoon olive oil
100 g/4 oz mushrooms, finely chopped
1 garlic clove, crushed

For the coating:
50 g/2 oz fine wholemeal breadcrumbs
15 g/½ oz sesame seeds or chopped mixed nuts
1 egg, beaten, or 1 tablespoon soya flour mixed with 2 tablespoons water*

■ Preheat the oven to 190°C/375°F/Gas Mark 5.
■ Mix the mashed potato and cabbage together with the butter or vegan margarine* and season to taste with salt and pepper. Allow to cool.
■ Heat the oil in a small pan and fry the mushrooms and garlic for 5 minutes. Allow to cool.
■ Take one heaped tablespoon of the potato and cabbage mixture in your hand and put 1 teaspoon garlic mushrooms in the centre. Top with more of the potato mixture and gently shape into a patty, enclosing the mushrooms. Repeat until the mixture is used up – it should make 8 patties. Place on a lightly floured plate and chill.
■ Mix the breadcrumbs and sesame seeds or nuts in a shallow dish. Dip each patty into beaten egg or soya paste*, and then roll to coat in the breadcrumbs.
■ Place on a greased baking sheet and bake in the preheated oven for about 35–40 minutes, turning once, until golden.

Makes 8 patties

PER SERVING
■
228 kcals (956 kj)
Protein 7 g
Fat 10 g
Carbohydrate 28 g
Fibre 4 g

FARFALLE WITH MANGE TOUT, FLAGEOLET BEANS, COURGETTES AND MINT

This simple meal is an excellent combination of proteins from the pasta (grain) and flageolet beans (pulse). It is fresh and light in flavour and makes a good summertime meal.

350 g/12 oz farfalle pasta
175 g/6 oz mange tout, trimmed and
    shredded diagonally
400 g/14 oz can chopped tomatoes
175 g/6 oz courgettes, diced
400-g/14-oz can of flageolet beans,
    drained
3 tablespoons chopped mint
salt and freshly ground black pepper
150 g/5 oz low-fat mozzarella
    cheese, cubed (omit for vegan*)
50 g/2 oz stoned olives, chopped
garlic bread, to serve (optional)

PER SERVING
■
263 kcals (1297 kj)
Protein 20 g
Fat 10.5 g
Carbohydrate 35.5 g
Fibre 4 g

■ Cook the pasta in a pan of boiling, lightly salted water, according to the instructions on the packet, until just tender and al dente. Drain and keep warm.

■ Steam the mange tout for 2 minutes and then drain and refresh under cold running water.

■ Drain the canned tomatoes and place in a saucepan with the courgettes and cook gently for 5 minutes. Stir in the mange tout and flageolet beans and heat through.

■ Add the cooked pasta and mozzarella, if using, then mix well and season to taste. Turn into a serving dish and sprinkle the chopped olives over the top. Serve with crusty garlic bread, if liked.

Serves 4

VEGAN

PENNE WITH
BROCCOLI, AVOCADO
AND ROAST PEPPER

PER SERVING
■
317 kcals (1320 kj)
Protein 8 g
Fat 20 g
Carbohydrate 27.5 g
Fibre 5 g

Pasta has a high fibre and protein content, and whereas avocado is high in fat it is also a good source of vitamin C. This recipe is quick and easy to prepare, making it perfect for a weekday meal.

350 g/12 oz penne pasta
225 g/8 oz broccoli, trimmed and separated into florets
1 red pepper, quartered and deseeded
1 small onion, finely chopped
1 tablespoon olive oil
1 tablespoon tarragon vinegar
1 tablespoon shoyu

4 gherkins, finely chopped
12 olives, stoned and halved
1 tablespoon chopped fresh coriander
1 tablespoon vegan pesto
1 avocado, peeled, stoned and sliced
25 g/1 oz pine nuts
salt and pepper
sprigs of coriander, to garnish

■ Cook the pasta in boiling water, according to the instructions on the packet, until just tender and al dente. Drain and keep warm.

■ Meanwhile, steam the broccoli florets for 6–8 minutes, and grill the red pepper, skin-side up, until blackened. Peel and then slice the flesh.

■ Gently fry the onion in the olive oil until soft and transluscent. Stir in the vinegar, shoyu, gherkins, olives, coriander and pesto. Add the broccoli, red pepper, avocado and pine nuts. Season to taste with salt and pepper. Mix well to coat and reheat gently for 2–3 minutes.

■ Stir in the hot pasta and transfer to a serving dish. Garnish with sprigs of coriander and serve immediately.

Serves 4

Opposite: Penne with broccoli, avocado and roast pepper

ASPARAGUS
FETTUCCINE STIR-FRY WITH PEANUT SAUCE

PER SERVING
■
295 kcals (1230 kj)
Protein 11 g
Fat 16 g
Carbohydrate 27 g
Fibre 5 g

Asparagus is high in vitamin C and beta-carotene. Although you can buy imported asparagus for much of the year, it is at its best during the early summer when it is in season.

350 g/12 oz fettuccine pasta
225 g/8 oz asparagus, trimmed and
   cut into 2.5-cm/1-inch pieces
225 g/8 oz thin green beans, cut into
   2.5-cm/1-inch pieces
1 tablespoon groundnut oil
1 large red chilli, deseeded and finely
   chopped
1 garlic clove, chopped
2.5-cm/1-inch fresh root ginger,
   peeled and chopped

4 spring onions, chopped
2 tablespoons water
2 tablespoons shoyu
2 tablespoons crunchy peanut butter
15 g/½ oz basil leaves, torn
1 tablespoon toasted sesame oil
25 g/1 oz plain peanuts, roasted and
   chopped
extra basil leaves, to garnish

■ Cook the pasta in a large pan of boiling, lightly salted water, according to the instructions on the packet, until just tender and al dente. Drain and keep warm.

■ Steam the asparagus and green beans for 5 minutes.

■ Heat the oil in a wok and quickly fry the chilli, garlic, ginger and spring onions for 1 minute. Add the asparagus and green beans, mix well and cook for 2 minutes.

■ Cream the water, shoyu and peanut butter together and stir into the vegetables with the basil and sesame oil. Add the warm pasta and toss well to combine. Turn into a serving dish and sprinkle with the peanuts. Garnish with basil leaves and serve.

Serves 4

MILLET PILAF

VEGAN

Usually a pilaf will be made with rice, but millet works very well as a substitute and adds variety to your diet. Broad beans are in season from late spring to early summer, but frozen broad beans are also excellent, making this a tasty all-year-round dish.

1 tablespoon olive oil

1 large onion, chopped

175 g/6 oz millet

2 teaspoons ground coriander

good pinch of ground cardamom

600 ml/1 pint vegetable stock

225 g/8 oz broccoli, separated into florets

100 g/4 oz sweetcorn kernels

100 g/4 oz broad beans, cooked

50 g/2 oz sultanas

salt and freshly ground black pepper

2 teaspoons grated orange zest

2 teaspoons chopped chives or spring onions

25 g/1 oz flaked almonds, toasted

PER SERVING
■
329 kcals (1380 kj)
Protein 12 g
Fat 9 g
Carbohydrate 53 g
Added sugar 2 g
Fibre 4.5 g

■ In a large saucepan, heat the olive oil over a medium heat and fry the onion for 5 minutes. Add the millet, coriander and cardamom. Stir and cook for 1 minute.

■ Add the stock, bring to the boil, then reduce the heat and simmer, covered, for 20 minutes.

■ Add the broccoli and cook for 5 minutes before adding the sweetcorn, broad beans, grated orange zest and sultanas. Stir well and then cook, covered, for a final 5 minutes.

■ Check the seasoning and serve, scattered with chives or spring onions and toasted flaked almonds.

Serves 4

*CAN BE VEGAN

WILD MUSHROOM
RISOTTO

PER SERVING
■
624 kcals (2636 kj)
Protein 16 g
Fat 11 g
Carbohydrate 117 g
Fibre 1 g

This would make an excellent healthy main course for a dinner party if served with the Wild Flower and Herb Salad (see page 92) and topped with Onion Marmalade (see page 103). The liquid from soaking the ceps is full of flavour. It is a good idea to strain it through fine muslin before adding it to a dish as there can be a gritty residue from the mushrooms.

1 litre/1¾ pints vegetable stock
2 teaspoons olive oil
1 onion, finely chopped
350 g/12 oz arborio rice
150 ml/¼ pint dry white wine
15 g/½ oz dried ceps
15 g/½ oz vegan margarine* or
    butter

225 g/8 oz mixed wild mushrooms,
    sliced
100 g/4 oz wild rice, cooked
50 g/2 oz Camargue red wild rice,
    cooked
50 g/2 oz vegetarian pecorino
    cheese (optional – omit for
    vegan*)
salt and freshly ground black pepper

■ Bring the stock to the boil in a large saucepan and keep it simmering.

■ Meanwhile, heat the oil in another large saucepan and fry the onion over a low heat until soft and just starting to colour. Add the arborio rice and cook for 2 minutes, stirring all the time.

■ Pour in the wine and cook for 5 minutes. Start adding the stock, using a large ladle. Cook gently, stirring regularly and making sure that all the stock has been absorbed before adding the next ladleful. This should take about 25–30 minutes.

■ While the rice is cooking, cover the ceps with boiling water and soak for about 15–20 minutes. Drain, reserving the soaking liquid and chop.

■ Heat the butter or vegan margarine* in a frying pan and quickly cook the sliced wild mushrooms for about 5 minutes.

■ Add all the mushrooms to the rice, together with the two cooked wild rices and the reserved soaking liquid. Add a little more stock if necessary and heat through thoroughly.

■ Remove from the heat and, if using, stir in the pecorino cheese. Season to taste and serve immediately.

Serves 4

Opposite: Wild mushroom risotto with Wild flower and herb salad (page 92)

VEGETABLE AND
BLACK EYE BEAN BANGALORE

PER SERVING

■

233 kcals (983 kj)
Protein 11 g
Fat 6 g
Carbohydrate 36 g
Fibre 4.5 g

Black eye beans are one of the few pulses that don't need soaking before cooking so they are a useful store cupboard ingredient.

100 g/4 oz black eye beans
1 tablespoon vegetable oil
1 onion, sliced
100 g/4 oz carrots, sliced
100 g/4 oz potatoes, cubed, washed and dried on kitchen paper
2 green chillies, sliced
2.5-cm/1-inch piece of cinnamon stick
6 whole cloves
6 green cardamons
2 teaspoons cumin seeds
1 teaspoon ground cumin
1 teaspoon ground coriander

¼ teaspoon turmeric
2.5-cm/1-inch fresh root ginger, peeled and grated
1 bay leaf
100 g/4 oz thin green beans, sliced
100 g/4 oz courgettes, sliced
175 ml/6 fl oz water
100 g/4 oz pineapple, peeled and cut into cubes
1 banana, sliced
salt, to taste
150 ml/5 fl oz natural low-fat yogurt or soya yogurt*
fresh coriander leaves, to garnish

■ Place the dry black eye beans in a saucepan. Cover with water, bring to the boil and then simmer for about 30 minutes or until the beans are tender. Drain.

■ Heat the oil in a large saucepan and fry the onion, carrots, potatoes and chillies for 5 minutes, stirring. Add all the spices and the ginger and cook for a further 2 minutes.

■ Add the bay leaf, green beans, courgettes and water. Cover and cook until the vegetables are tender (about 15 minutes).

■ Add the pineapple, banana, black eye beans and yogurt and gently heat through. Season to taste with salt and serve on a bed of rice, garnished with coriander leaves.

Serves 4

MUSHROOM, PEPPER
AND TOMATO STEW
WITH QUINOA

VEGAN

Quinoa is an excellent source of protein. It is an ancient grain which has recently regained popularity in the West and makes a good alternative to bulgar wheat or cous cous.

1 tablespoon vegetable oil

225 g/8 oz baby onions or shallots, halved

675 g/1½ lb mixed mushrooms (button, oyster, chestnut, etc.), wiped and quartered if large

2 garlic cloves, chopped

sprig of rosemary

3 tablespoons shoyu

25 g/1 oz dark muscovado sugar

2 teaspoons yeast extract

300 ml/½ pint vegetable stock

1 red pepper, deseeded and cut into thin strips

400-g/14-oz can of chopped tomatoes

salt and freshly ground black pepper

2 teaspoons arrowroot

225 g/8 oz quinoa, cooked and kept warm

handful of chopped parsley, to garnish

PER SERVING

■

313 kcals (1319 kj)
Protein 15 g
Fat 7 g
Carbohydrate 50 g
Fibre 4 g

■ Heat the oil in a large saucepan and fry the onions until starting to brown. Stir in the mushrooms, garlic and sprig of rosemary and cook over a high heat until the mushrooms start to release their juices.

■ In a bowl, mix together the shoyu, sugar and yeast extract, which has been dissolved in the stock. Season well and add to the mushroooms with the red pepper and tomatoes. Simmer for 20–30 minutes until half of the liquid has evaporated.

■ In a small bowl or cup, mix the arrowroot with a little water to make a paste. Add to the stew, then bring to the boil, stirring. Reduce the heat and simmer for 1 minute to thicken. Remove the sprig of rosemary and check the seasoning.

■ Put the cooked quinoa on a serving platter and spoon the stew over the top. Sprinkle with lots of chopped parsley and serve.

Serves 4

NUTTY FLAN WITH
TOFU AND VEGETABLE FILLING

Tofu can be used as a substitute for cream and eggs in flans. This recipe is good if you don't like making pastry as no rolling out is involved. To make a vegan version, omit the cheese and oil from the flan case and use 50 g/2 oz vegan margarine rubbed into the mixture. It will be more crumbly than the cheese version, but still tasty.

PER SERVING

■

389 kcals (1620 kj)
Protein 16 g
Carbohydrate 24 g
Fat 26 g
Fibre 5 g

Flan case:
50 g/2 oz ground almonds
50 g/2 oz low-fat vegetarian
   Cheddar cheese, finely grated
50 g/2 oz wholemeal breadcrumbs
25 g/1 oz chopped roast hazelnuts
1 teaspoon dried mixed herbs
¼ teaspoon cayenne pepper
   (optional)
2 tablespoons groundnut oil

Filling:
2 onions, cut into bite-sized chunks
100 g/4 oz carrots, sliced into
   2.5-cm/1-inch lengths

1 red pepper, deseeded and chopped
   into 2.5-cm/1-inch pieces
100 g/4 oz sweet potato, chopped
   into 2.5-cm/1-inch cubes
1 tablespoon olive oil
200 g/7 oz silken tofu
1 tablespoon cider vinegar
1 teaspoon each of dried rosemary,
   sage and thyme, ground together
   in a pestle and mortar
150 ml/¼ pint skimmed or soya milk
salt and freshly ground black pepper
1 tablespoon sunflower seeds

■ Preheat the oven to 200°C/400°F/Gas Mark 6.

■ Mix all the ingredients for the flan case together and press into a 17-cm/ 7-inch loose-bottomed flan ring. Bake in the preheated oven for 10 minutes.

■ Put all the vegetables in a roasting pan, drizzle the oil over and toss well. Roast in the preheated oven for about 30–40 minutes, turning several times, until tender and golden.

■ Put the tofu, cider vinegar, dried herbs and milk into a blender or food processor and blend until smooth. Season well.

■ Put the roast vegetables in the flan case, then spoon the tofu mixture evenly over the top. Sprinkle sunflower seeds over the surface and bake for 20–25 minutes.

■ Turn out onto a serving plate and serve with a green salad or seasonal vegetables.

Serves 6

Opposite: Nutty flan with tofu and vegetable filling

SWEET AND SOUR
CABBAGE PARCELS

*CAN BE VEGAN

Tying up the cabbage leaves with chives makes this nutritious dish look like little Christmas parcels.

PER SERVING
■
194 kcals (806 kj)
Protein 5 g
Fat 11 g
Carbohydrate 20 g
Added sugar 3 g
Fibre 5 g

4 large leaves from a Savoy cabbage
1 tablespoon olive oil
1 small onion, finely chopped
1 garlic clove, crushed
100 g/4 oz mushrooms, chopped
25 g/1 oz toasted pine kernels
1 teaspoon wholegrain mustard
1 tablespoon shoyu or tamari sauce
pinch of dried sage and thyme
salt and freshly ground black pepper
long chives
a little vegetable stock

Sweet and sour peppers:
1 tablespoon olive oil
1 large onion, cut in half and thinly
  sliced
2 garlic cloves, crushed
2 red peppers, deseeded and
  shredded into long thin strips
2 yellow peppers, deseeded and
  shredded into long thin strips
200-g/7-oz can of chopped tomatoes
1 tablespoon tomato purée
2 tablespoons cider vinegar
1 tablespoon honey or maple syrup*
1 tablespoon balsamic vinegar
salt and freshly ground black pepper

■ Preheat the oven to 180°C/350°F/Gas Mark 4. Remove the base of the stem from each cabbage leaf, and blanch the leaves for 4–5 minutes to soften.

■ Heat the oil in a saucepan and fry the onion and garlic for a few minutes until starting to colour. Add the mushrooms and cook gently for 5 minutes. Stir in the pine kernels, mustard, shoyu or tamari, sage, thyme and seasoning.

■ Divide the mixture between the cabbage leaves and roll up tightly, tucking in the sides. Use chives to tie each one (criss-cross style) to look like a parcel.

■ Place in an ovenproof dish, add a little vegetable stock, cover with foil and bake in the preheated oven for 45–50 minutes.

■ Meanwhile, heat the oil and fry the onion, garlic and peppers for 5 minutes until softening. Add the tomatoes, tomato purée, cider vinegar and honey or maple syrup*, and bring to the boil. Remove from the heat, add the balsamic vinegar and season. Remove half of the mixture with a slotted spoon and reserve. Blend the remaining mixture, with all the juices, to a smooth sauce.

■ Gently reheat the reserved peppers and the sauce in separate saucepans. Put a mound of the pepper mixture on each warm serving plate. Place a cabbage parcel on top, then drizzle the pepper sauce on the plate around it.

Serves 4

ENCHILADAS WITH
WARM TOMATO SALSA

VEGAN

If you can't get black beans, kidney beans or pinto beans work well in this Mexican-style dish.

1 tablespoon groundnut oil
1 onion, halved and sliced
1 red chilli, finely chopped
1 teaspoon ground coriander
100 g/4 oz black beans, cooked
100 g/4 oz sweetcorn kernels
   (defrosted if using frozen)
1 tablespoon chopped fresh
   coriander
juice of 1 lime
salt and freshly ground black pepper
4 large soft flour tortillas

For the salsa:
1 tablespoon tomato purée
4 tablespoons water
1 small red onion, finely chopped
1 garlic clove, crushed
4 ripe tomatoes, roughly chopped
1 tablespoon chopped fresh
   coriander

PER SERVING
■

255 kcals (1081 kj)
Protein 10.5 g
Fat 4 g
Carbohydrate 47 g
Fibre 6 g

■ Preheat the oven to 180°C/350°F/Gas Mark 4.

■ Heat the oil and fry the onion and chilli until tender. Add the ground coriander and cook for 2 minutes. Stir in the cooked black beans, sweetcorn, coriander and lime juice and stir thoroughly to heat through. Season to taste and keep warm.

■ Wrap the tortillas in foil and warm through in the preheated oven for 10 minutes.

■ To make the salsa, put the tomato purée and water in a small saucepan with the onion and garlic. Stir and cook for 10 minutes. Add the chopped tomatoes and coriander and mix well. Remove from the heat.

■ Divide the filling between the 4 tortillas and fold each one over in half to make a semicircular shape. Spoon the warm salsa over the top of each and serve with a green salad.

Serves 4

SZECHUAN TOFU

Szechuan (Sichuan) pepper, although hot and spicy, is not really a variety of pepper at all but the dried berries and husks from a type of ash tree. It is one of the ingredients in Chinese five-spice powder.

225 g/8 oz long-grain rice
2 teaspoons groundnut oil
1 garlic clove, peeled
2.5-cm/1-inch piece fresh root ginger, peeled
2 dried red chillies
1 tablespoon szechuan peppercorns
1 onion, chopped
1 green pepper, sliced
225 g/8 oz marinated tofu pieces
225 g/8 oz mushrooms, sliced
225 g/8 oz broccoli florets
2 tablespoons vegetable stock
2 tablespoons shoyu
50 g/2 oz cashew nuts, toasted

■ Cook the rice, according to the packet instructions, and keep warm if necessary.
■ Heat the oil in a wok. Use a rolling pin to bruise the garlic and ginger. When the oil is hot, add the garlic, ginger and chillies and allow to sizzle for 5 minutes. Remove with a slotted spoon and discard.
■ Meanwhile, dry-roast the szechuan peppercorns and grind in a pestle and mortar or grinder attachment. Add to the wok with the onion and green pepper and cook for 5 minutes. Add the tofu, mushrooms and broccoli and cook for 5 minutes, then add the stock and shoyu and allow to simmer for 5–10 minutes until the vegetables are tender but still crisp.
■ Stir in the toasted cashew nuts and serve on a bed of rice.

Serves 4

Opposite: Szechuan tofu

MARINATED TOFU
AND VEGETABLE FILO PIE

Tofu is a versatile ingredient and in addition to being one of the best vegetarian protein sources it also gives substance to a meal.

PER SERVING

■

355 kcals (1483 kj)
Protein 22 g
Fat 15 g
Carbohydrate 34 g
Added sugar 0.6 g
Fibre 5 g

1 teaspoon olive oil
100 g/4 oz leeks, trimmed and sliced
1 garlic clove, crushed
pinch of chilli powder
100 g/4 oz carrots, diced
100 g/4 oz parsnips, diced
100 g/4 oz swede, diced
100 g/4 oz thin green beans, frozen
225 g/8 oz marinated tofu pieces
100 g/4 oz tomatoes, skinned and chopped
1 tablespoon tomato purée
300 ml/½ pint vegetable stock
salt and pepper
1 tablespoon plain white flour
3 sheets filo pastry, or 100 g/4 oz depending on the size of sheet
15 g/½ oz vegan margarine, melted

■ Preheat the oven to 200°C/400°F/Gas Mark 6.
■ Heat the oil in a large saucepan and sweat the leeks and garlic together, with the lid on, for 5 minutes. Add the chilli powder, carrots, parsnips, swede and green beans and cook gently for 10 minutes.
■ Add the tofu pieces, tomatoes, tomato purée and vegetable stock and cook gently until the vegetables are tender. Season well. Sprinkle the flour over and stir to mix. Cool and transfer to a pie dish.
■ Brush one sheet of filo pastry with melted margarine and place over the vegetables. Trim to size. Repeat with the remaining 2 sheets. Scrunch up the pastry trimmings roughly and scatter over the top. Bake in the preheated oven for 20 minutes until golden. Serve immediately.

Serves 4

BROAD BEAN AND
SWEETCORN STEW

VEGAN

Stews are usually associated with winter but this one uses summer vegetables. However, you could substitute frozen vegetables when fresh ones are out of season. Bulgar wheat gives the stew bulk.

PER SERVING
■
565 kcals (2369 kj)
Protein 20 g
Fat 7 g
Carbohydrate 109 g
Added sugar 4 g
Fibre 10 g

1 teaspoon olive oil

1 onion, chopped

1 red chilli, finely chopped

1 tablespoon fresh oregano

400-g/14-oz can of chopped tomatoes

450 g/1 lb broad beans (shelled weight)

225 g/8 oz sweetcorn kernels

225 g/8 oz carrots, sliced

450 ml/15 fl oz vegetable stock

100 g/4 oz bulgar wheat

grated zest and juice of 1 lemon

salt and freshly ground black pepper

2 tablespoons chopped parsley

jacket potatoes and a fresh green salad, to serve

■ Heat the oil in a large saucepan and cook the onion, chilli and oregano until the onion has softened. Add the tomatoes, broad beans, sweetcorn, carrots and vegetable stock and bring to the boil.

■ Add the bulgar wheat and simmer for about 15–20 minutes until the vegetables and bulgar wheat are cooked. Stir in the lemon juice and zest.

■ Season to taste with salt and pepper and sprinkle with chopped parsley. Serve with jacket potatoes and a green salad.

Serves 4

PATATAS BRAVAS

PER SERVING
■
163 kcals (686 kj)
Protein 4 g
Fat 3 g
Carbohydrate 31 g
Fibre 3 g

Potatoes and parsley are both good sources of vitamin C. This spicy combination makes a good side dish.

1 tablespoon groundnut oil
675 g/1½ lb cooked cubed potatoes
1 onion, finely chopped
1 teaspoon chilli powder

2–3 tablespoons tomato purée
1 tablespoon chopped parsley, to
  garnish

■ Heat the oil in a non-stick frying pan. Gently fry the potatoes, onion and chilli powder together for about 10 minutes until the vegetables are golden. Stir in the tomato purée.
■ Serve the potatoes as a side dish, garnished with chopped parsley.

Serves 4

SPICED RED CABBAGE

PER SERVING
■
72 kcals (299 kj)
Protein 2 g
Fat 3 g
Carbohydrate 9 g
Fibre 4 g

Sunflower oil is lighter in flavour than olive oil, is high in polyunsaturates and a good source of vitamin E.

1 tablespoon sunflower oil
1 onion, chopped
450 g/1 lb red cabbage, shredded
225 g/8 oz cooking apples, peeled,
  cored and diced

2.5-cm/1-inch piece fresh root
  ginger, peeled and grated
pinch of ground cinnamon or allspice
150 ml/¼ pint vegetable stock
salt and freshly ground black pepper

■ Heat the oil in a large saucepan. Add the onion, red cabbage and apple and cook gently for 5 minutes. Add the ginger and cinnamon or allspice and the vegetable stock.
■ Bring to the boil, then reduce the heat and simmer gently for 15–20 minutes until most of the liquid has evaporated and the vegetables are tender. Season to taste and serve.

Serves 4 as a side dish

Opposite: Patatas Bravas and Spiced red cabbage

QUICK-FRIED
SHREDDED KOHLRABI

Kohlrabi looks so strange that it can be difficult to think what to do with it! However, this unusual vegetable can be sliced and boiled like a turnip or stir-fried with other flavoursome ingredients.

1 tablespoon vegetable oil
225 g/8 oz kohlrabi, peeled and grated
1 onion, halved and sliced

2.5-cm/1-inch piece fresh root ginger, peeled and grated
dash of Tabasco
salt and freshly ground black pepper

■ Heat the oil in a non-stick frying pan. Gently fry the kohlrabi and onion for about 10 minutes until tender. Add the ginger and stir well to warm through.
■ Season with Tabasco and salt and pepper to taste and serve immediately.

Serves 4 as a side dish

SWEET BAKED
BEETROOT

Beetroot is high in Vitamins A, C and K, and also in the minerals iron and calcium. This is a delicious way to prepare this often forgotten vegetable.

675 g/1½ lb raw beetroot, peeled and quartered
2 red onions, peeled and quartered
2 tablespoons olive oil

1 tablespoon honey or maple syrup*
salt and freshly ground black pepper
1 tablespoon balsamic vinegar

■ Preheat the oven to 180°C/350°F/Gas Mark 4.
■ Place the beetroot and onion quarters in a roasting pan.
■ Mix the olive oil and honey or maple syrup* together and season well. Pour over the vegetables and toss to coat.
■ Roast in the preheated oven for about 45–60 minutes until the beetroot is tender. Sprinkle with the balsamic vinegar and toss well. Serve immediately..

Serves 4 as a side dish

CELERIAC MASH

Awarming, starchy side dish. If you want to reduce the fat content, use less (or no) margarine when mashing the mixture.

450 g/1 lb potatoes, peeled and
    cubed
450 g/1 lb celeriac, peeled and cubed
50 g/2 oz vegan margarine
2 sticks celery, very finely chopped

2 garlic cloves, crushed
2 tablespoons fresh basil or
    coriander, chopped
salt and pepper

PER SERVING
■
203 kcals (848 kj)
Protein 4 g
Fat 11 g
Carbohydrate 23 g
Fibre 6 g

■ Boil the potato and celeriac together until tender. Drain and mash.
■ Meanwhile, heat the margarine in a frying pan and gently cook the celery and garlic until tender. Stir into the mashed potato, add the herbs and season.

Serves 4

TERIYAKI STIR-FRY

Teriyaki sauce contains honey so it is not suitable for a vegan diet, but you could use the tempeh marinade on page 90 instead.

225 g/8 oz egg-free noodles
1 tablespoon groundnut oil
1 onion, sliced
1 garlic clove, crushed
100 g/4 oz broccoli florets
100 g/4 oz asparagus spears, cut into
    2.5-cm/1-inch lengths and
    steamed

50 g/2 oz baby sweetcorn, halved
50 g/2 oz mange tout, trimmed and
    halved
100 g/4 oz thin green beans, cut into
    2.5-cm/1-inch lengths
175 g/6 oz beansprouts
3 tablespoons teriyaki sauce
100 g/4 oz cherry tomatoes, halved

PER SERVING
■
117 kcals (490 kj)
Protein 7 g
Fat 4 g
Carbohydrate 15 g
Fibre 3 g

■ Cook the noodles, according to the instructions on the packet. Drain and keep warm.
■ Heat the oil in a wok. Add the onion and garlic and cook for 2 minutes. Add the broccoli and cauliflower and cook for 6 minutes. Add the asparagus, sweetcorn, mange tout and green beans and continue stir-frying for 3 minutes.
■ Stir in the beansprouts and teriyaki sauce and serve on a bed of noodles, garnished with the cherry tomatoes.

Serves 4

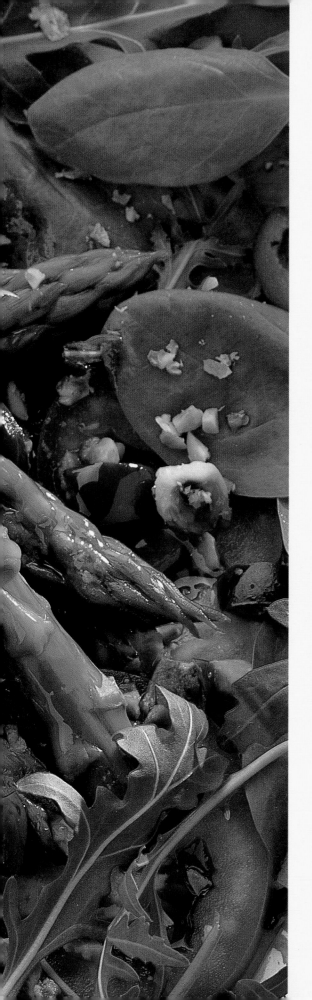

SALADS,
DRESSINGS
AND RELISHES

Mixed grain tabbouleh salad
Sprouting bean salad with ginger dressing
Apricot and chick pea salad
Spicy bean salad
Mixed potato salad
Japanese sea vegetable salad
Beetroot salad with toasted seeds
Rice noodle salad with oriental vegetables
Marinated tempeh and baby vegetable salad
  with tofu mayonnaise
Wild flower and herb salad
Italian grilled pepper salad
Asparagus salad with hazelnut dressing
Mixed green salad with tofu and mango
Walnut dressing
Spinach and mint salad with garlic croutons
Thai tofu dip
Sun-dried tomato dip
Teriyaki dressing
Sweetcorn salsa
Cucumber, apple, onion and mint relish
Banana, onion and tomato chutney
Fresh orange and date chutney
Courgette relish
Onion marmalade

Left: Asparagus salad with hazelnut dressing (page 94)

VEGAN

MIXED GRAIN
TABBOULEH SALAD

Using a mixture of grains gives variety of texture and flavour to this popular salad. If you wish to make it healthier still, reduce the amount of olive oil and substitute a little more lemon juice.

PER SERVING

■

149 kcals (620 kj)
Protein 3 g
Fat 8 g
Carbohydrate 17 g
Fibre 2 g

50 g/2 oz millet, cooked
50 g/2 oz bulgar wheat, cooked
½ green pepper, deseeded and finely diced
½ red pepper, finely diced
½ carrot, very finely diced
6 spring onions, finely chopped
¼ cucumber, very finely diced
2 tomatoes, skinned and finely diced
4 tablespoons fruity olive oil
1 garlic clove, crushed
3 tablespoons lemon juice
2 tablespoons chopped parsley
2 tablespoons chopped mint
salt and freshly ground black pepper

■ Combine the two cooked grains in a bowl and mix in the peppers, carrot, spring onions, cucumber and tomatoes.

■ In a separate bowl, mix the olive oil, garlic, lemon juice, parsley and mint and season to taste.

■ Pour over the salad ingredients and mix well. Chill in the refrigerator before serving.

Serves 6

SPROUTING
BEAN SALAD WITH GINGER DRESSING

VEGAN

When beans and seeds are sprouting, they are at their most nutritious and are an excellent ingredient to include in your diet, either raw or stir-fried. Chick peas, mung beans, aduki beans, alfalfa and fenugreek seeds make an interesting mixture and you can sprout them in a jam jar in a few days so that you have an almost constant and inexpensive supply of them.

PER SERVING

■

48 kcals (201 kj)
Protein 3 g
Fat 0.7 g
Carbohydrate 8 g
Fibre 2 g

225 g/8 oz mixed sprouting beans
I red pepper, deseeded and finely sliced
I stick celery, shredded
I red onion, finely sliced
¼ cucumber, quartered, then sliced
50 g/2 oz watercress, washed and chopped

Ginger dressing:
5-cm/2-in piece fresh root ginger, grated and juice squeezed out
I tablespoon shoyu
juice of I lime
I garlic clove, crushed
salt and pepper to taste

■ Mix all the salad ingredients together in a bowl.
■ Make the dressing by mixing the ginger juice, shoyu, lime juice and garlic together. Season to taste.
■ Pour the dressing over the salad, toss well and serve immediately.

Serves 4

Apricot and
CHICK PEA SALAD

PER SERVING

■

483 kcals (2021 kj)
Protein 14 g
Fat 9 g
Carbohydrate 88 g
Fibre 3 g

Dried apricots are a good source of iron and their flavour complements the slight earthiness of the chick peas to make a delicious and unusual salad. Served with cubes of grilled smoked tofu, this would make a good light lunch.

100 g/4 oz bulgar wheat
100 g/4 oz cooked chick peas
50 g/2 oz sprouted chick peas/mixed
  beansprouts
50 g/2 oz ready-to-eat apricots,
  chopped
25 g/1 oz toasted, flaked almonds
2 tablespoons chopped parsley
sprigs of parsley, to garnish

Dressing:
1 tablespoon groundnut oil
1 small onion, finely chopped
1 teaspoon crushed dried chillies
1 teaspoon ground cumin
pinch ground cinnamon
pinch ground cloves
salt and pepper

■ Pour boiling water over the bulgar wheat and leave to stand for 30 minutes, then drain. Fluff up the grains with a fork.

■ Mix together the bulgar wheat, chick peas, sprouted chick peas, apricots, almonds and parsley in a bowl.

■ To make the dressing, heat the oil in a saucepan and fry the onion until soft. Add the spices and cook for 2 minutes. Season to taste and stir into the salad immediately while the dressing is still warm. Garnish with sprigs of parsley and serve.

Serves 4

Opposite: Apricot and chick pea salad

SPICY BEAN SALAD

A spicy variation on the traditional three-bean salad, this dish is very high in protein.

1 teaspoon vegetable oil
1 onion, finely chopped
2 teaspoons garam masala
1/2 teaspoon chilli powder
400-g/14-oz can of kidney beans,
  rinsed and drained

400-g/14-oz can of butterbeans,
  rinsed and drained
175 g/6 oz thin green beans, cooked
crisp lettuce leaves, shredded, to
  serve

■ Heat the oil in a saucepan and fry the onion until soft. Add the garam masala and chilli powder and cook for 2 minutes.

■ Add all the beans and heat through, stirring to coat. Remove from the heat and cool.

■ Serve on a bed of shredded crisp lettuce leaves.

Serves 4

MIXED POTATO SALAD

This salad is high in starchy carbohydrate and makes an excellent side dish in both summer and winter.

375 g/12 oz potatoes, cubed
375 g/12 oz sweet potatoes, cubed
100 g/4 oz green beans
1 small red onion, finely sliced
3 ripe tomatoes, skinned and
  chopped

1 tablespoon fruity olive oil
1 tablespoon lemon juice
1 tablespoon chopped oregano
salt and freshly ground black pepper

■ Cook the potatoes and sweet potatoes in a pan of boiling water until tender. Drain.

■ Cook the green beans in boiling water, then drain and add to the potatoes with the onion and tomatoes.

■ Mix the olive oil, lemon juice and oregano together. Season to taste and pour over the salad while still warm. Put into a salad bowl and serve.

Serves 4

JAPANESE SEA
VEGETABLE SALAD

Sea vegetables are full of vitamins and minerals, but in most recipes you need only use a tiny pinch as once soaked they expand to four or five times their original volume.

pinch of dried arame or hiziki
225 g/8 oz beansprouts, washed and drained
½ cucumber, halved lengthways and finely sliced
50 g/2 oz mange tout, trimmed and shredded
50 g/2 oz carrots, cut into long thin strips
4 tablespoons rice vinegar
1 tablespoon shoyu
1 teaspoon caster sugar
¼–½ teaspoon wasabi (Japanese horseradish)
pinch of salt
1 tablespoon sesame seeds, dry toasted

■ Soak the arame or hiziki in cold water for 10 minutes to reconstitute. Drain.
■ Mix the arame, beansprouts, cucumber, mange tout and carrots together in a bowl.
■ Mix together the rice vinegar, shoyu, caster sugar, wasabi paste and salt, and pour over the salad just before serving. Toss all the ingredients together in the bowl, then sprinkle toasted sesame seeds over the top to garnish.

Serves 4

PER SERVING
■

57 kcals (239 kj)
Protein 3.5 g
Fat 2 g
Carbohydrate 7 g
Fibre 2 g

BEETROOT SALAD
WITH TOASTED SEEDS

PER SERVING
■
131 kcals (543 kj)
Protein 4 g
Fat 9.5 g
Carbohydrate 7.5 g
Fibre 3 g

If you want to cut down on the fat in your diet, you could try reducing the fat in this recipe to 1 teaspoon sesame oil to give just a hint of its distinctive flavour in the dressing.

225 g/8 oz raw beetroot, grated
6 spring onions, shredded
2 sticks celery, shredded
50 g/2 oz baby spinach leaves
1 tablespoon pumpkin seeds
1 tablespoon sunflower seeds
1 tablespoon sesame seeds

For the dressing:
2 tablespoons red wine vinegar
1 tablespoon sesame oil
2 teaspoons groundnut oil
1 tablespoon shoyu or tamari
1 tablespoon chopped mint
salt and pepper

■ Make the dressing by stirring all the ingredients together.
■ Mix the grated beetroot, spring onions and celery together in a bowl and pour the dressing over, mixing well to coat.
■ Arrange the spinach leaves on a serving platter, then pile the beetroot mixture on top, leaving a border of spinach leaves showing.
■ In a heavy-based, non-stick pan, dry-roast the seeds until golden and popping. Scatter over the salad and serve.

Serves 4

RICE NOODLE SALAD
WITH ORIENTAL VEGETABLES

A low fat salad, with quickly stir-fried vegetables to preserve the nutritional content.

50 g/2 oz rice noodles
1 tablespoon groundnut oil
25 g/1 oz baby sweetcorn halved
25 g/1 oz mange tout, trimmed and sliced diagonally
3 spring onions, shredded diagonally
5-cm/2-in piece daikon, peeled and grated
25 g/1 oz shitake mushrooms, sliced
1 quantity of Teriyaki Dressing (see page 99)
pinch of arame, soaked and drained
25 g/1 oz peanuts, roasted and chopped, to garnish

■ Cook the rice noodles according to the instructions on the packet. Drain and plunge immediately into cold water. When cold, drain. Chop into shorter lengths if preferred and place in a bowl.

■ Heat the oil in a frying pan and quickly stir-fry all the vegetables for 2–3 minutes. Remove from the heat.

■ Add the teriyaki dressing while the vegetables are still warm. Pour over the rice noodles and immediately toss well to coat. Leave to cool and add the arame.

■ Arrange on a serving platter and scatter the peanuts over the top. Allow to cool and serve.

Serves 4

> **PER SERVING (EXCLUDING TERIYAKI DRESSING)**
> ■
> 109 kcals (454 kj)
> Protein 3 g
> Fat 6 g
> Carbohydrate 12 g
> Fibre 1 g

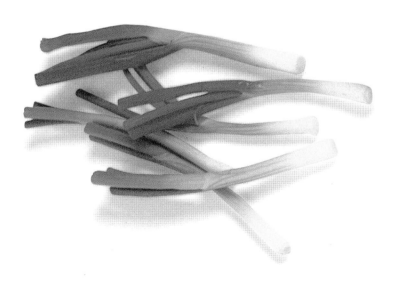

VEGAN

MARINATED TEMPEH
AND BABY VEGETABLE SALAD
WITH TOFU MAYONNAISE

PER SERVING
■

147 kcals (609 kj)
Protein 8 g
Fat 11 g
Carbohydrate 5 g
Fibre 2 g

Y ou can buy tempeh in the freezer section of health food shops or it is sometimes bottled in brine. Tempeh is a good source of protein as it is made from soya beans.

100 g/4 oz tempeh, defrosted
2 tablespoons shoyu or tamari
1 garlic clove, crushed
1 tablespoon groundnut oil
50 g/2 oz baby carrots, sliced
 lenthways
50 g/2 oz baby sweetcorn, halved
 lenthways
25 g/1 oz petit pois (frozen)
100 g/4 oz Chinese leaves, shredded

Tofu mayonnaise:
50 g/2 oz silken tofu
1 garlic clove, crushed
grated zest and juice of ½ lemon
2 tablespoons cold pressed
 sunflower oil
2 tablespoons water
15 g/½ oz fresh coriander, chopped
salt and freshly ground black pepper

VARIATIONS
■

Add one of the following flavourings to the tofu mayonnaise in place of the coriander:

■ 1 tablespoon chopped mixed herbs
■ 1 tablespoon vegetarian or vegan pesto
■ 2 tablespoons Sun-dried Tomato Dip (see page 99)
■ 1 heaped teaspoon capers and 1 large gherkin, finely chopped
■ 1 tablespoon sweet fruit chutney (e.g. mango, peach)
■ 1 teaspoon curry paste

■ Slice the tempeh into thin strips about 2.5 cm/1 in long.
■ Mix the shoyu or tamari with the garlic and toss the tempeh in the mixture. Leave to marinate for 30–60 minutes.
■ Remove the tempeh from the marinade with a slotted spoon. Toss in the oil, then cook under a medium grill for about 10 minutes until golden. Cool.
■ Meanwhile, steam the baby carrots and sweetcorn for 6–10 minutes until tender. Cook the petit pois in boiling water for 2–3 minutes until tender. Drain and cool.
■ Arrange the Chinese leaves on a platter. Mix the tempeh and vegetables together and scatter over the leaves.
■ For the mayonnaise, put all the ingredients except the coriander in a blender or food processor. Blend until smooth. If too thick, add a little more water or lemon juice. If too thin, add a little more tofu. Stir in the coriander and season to taste. Drizzle over the salad and serve.

Serves 4

Opposite: Marinated tempeh and baby vegetable salad with tofu mayonnaise

WILD FLOWER
AND HERB SALAD

This colourful and unusual salad is best made with herbs and flowers picked fresh from the garden on which no pesticides have been used. It goes well with Wild Mushroom Risotto (see page 64).

PER SERVING

■

63 kcals (261 kj)
Protein 2 g
Fat 4.5 g
Carbohydrate 4 g
Fibre 1 g

50 g/2 oz rocket leaves
50 g/2 oz baby spinach leaves
15 g/½ oz mint leaves
15 g/½ oz flat-leaf parsley
15 g/½ oz basil, roughly torn
small bunch of chives, chopped
a few chive flowers
a few oregano flowers
1 small red onion, halved and very
    finely sliced
225 g/8 oz cherry tomatoes, halved
12 nasturtium flowers (or other
    edible flowers), to garnish

Mustard dressing:
2 teaspoons dijon mustard
2 tablespoons tarragon or other
    herb vinegar
1 garlic clove, crushed
1 tablespoon fruity extra virgin olive
    oil
finely chopped zest of 1 lemon
salt and pepper

■ Mix the rocket, spinach, mint, parsley, basil, chives and the herb flowers in a large salad bowl. Scatter over the onion and cherry tomatoes and decorate with nasturtium flowers.

■ To make the dressing, whisk all the ingredients together in a small bowl (a balloon whisk is best). Pour into a small jug and serve with the salad.

Serves 4

ITALIAN GRILLED
PEPPER SALAD

Red and yellow peppers are high in beta-carotene. Add the raw salad vegetables too and this salad is not only full of vitamins, but low in calories and fat.

1 large cos lettuce
2 red peppers
2 green peppers
2 yellow peppers
225 g/8 oz cherry tomatoes, halved
15 g/½ oz basil leaves, roughly torn
1 tablespoon capers
50 g/2 oz olives, stoned and halved
1 tablespoon fruity olive oil
grated zest of 1 lemon
1 tablespoon balsamic vinegar
pinch of salt
25 g/1 oz vegetarian Parmesan or pecorino cheese (optional – omit for vegan*)

PER SERVING
■
94 kcals (393 kj)
Protein 4 g
Fat 5 g
Fibre 3.5 g

■ Shred the lettuce and arrange on a platter.
■ Cut the peppers into quarters and remove the seeds. Grill, skin-side up, until starting to char. Cut into strips and place in a bowl. Add the cherry tomatoes, basil leaves, capers and olives.
■ Mix the olive oil, lemon zest and juice, balsamic vinegar, salt and pepper together.
■ Toss the vegetables in the dressing and arrange on the bed of lettuce. Use a cheese parer to make thin slivers of Parmesan or pecorino, if using, and scatter over the salad. Serve with rustic, crusty, Italian bread.

Serves 6

ASPARAGUS SALAD
WITH HAZELNUT DRESSING

PER SERVING

■

135 kcals (557 kj)
Protein 3 g
Fat 11 g
Carbohydrate 5 g
Fibre 3 g

Although nuts and olives are high in fat, nuts are also a good protein source and olives add interest to the flavours in your diet. You can balance this out by serving this salad with a low-fat main course such as Farfalle with Mange Tout, Flageolet Beans, Courgettes and Mint (see page 59).

225 g/8 oz asparagus spears
25 g/1 oz baby spinach leaves
25 g/1 oz rocket leaves
450 g/1 lb tomatoes, sliced
2 tablespoons fruity olive oil
2 teaspoons hazelnut oil
1 tablespoon balsamic vinegar
salt and freshly ground black pepper
25 g/1 oz stoned black olives, roughly chopped
15 g/½ oz roasted chopped hazelnuts

■ Steam the asparagus spears for 6–10 minutes. As soon as they are tender, refresh under cold running water and then cut into 5-cm/2-in lengths.
■ Arrange the spinach and rocket leaves around the edge of a serving platter. Arrange the slices of tomato in a ring inside the leaves, leaving room in the centre of the plate for the asparagus spears. Place the cooled asparagus in the centre.
■ Mix the olive oil, hazelnut oil, balsamic vinegar and salt and pepper together and drizzle over the salad. Sprinkle with the chopped olives and toasted hazelnuts and serve.

Serves 4

Opposite: Asparagus salad with hazelnut dressing

MIXED GREEN SALAD
WITH TOFU AND MANGO

Fruit is a delicious addition to many salad mixtures, and mango, in particular, goes well with tofu. Baking the tofu changes its texture and adds to the interest of the salad.

100 g/4 oz iceberg lettuce, shredded
50 g/2 oz baby spinach leaves
50 g/2 oz watercress
4 spring onions, shredded
¼ cucumber, sliced
100 g/4 oz marinated tofu
1 tablespoon sunflower oil
2 mangoes, peeled, stoned and sliced

■ Preheat the oven to 200°C/400°F/Gas Mark 6. Preheat the grill.
■ Mix the salad leaves, onions and cucumber together and arrange on a platter. Chill in the refrigerator.
■ Cut the tofu into small cubes and toss in the oil. Place on a baking sheet and bake in the preheated oven for 20–30 minutes until golden and starting to crisp.
■ Place the slices of mango under the hot grill and cook, turning once, for about 6 minutes.
■ Scatter the tofu and mango over the green salad. Serve with either Walnut Dressing (below) or Teryaki Dressing (see page 99).

Serves 4

WALNUT DRESSING

1 tablespoon cold pressed sunflower oil
1 teaspoon walnut oil
juice of 1 lemon
15 g/½ oz walnuts, lightly toasted and chopped
salt and pepper

■ Mix all the ingredients together and serve with a green salad.

Serves 4

SPINACH AND MINT
SALAD WITH GARLIC CROUTONS

*CAN BE VEGAN

Mint comes in all sorts of flavours. For this salad, I like to pick a selection of spearmint, peppermint, applemint, ginger mint and pineapple mint. You can use whatever combination you like or a single variety if you prefer.

100 g/4 oz baby spinach leaves, washed
25 g/1 oz lamb's lettuce
15 g/½ oz mint leaves, roughly chopped
100 g/4 oz cherry tomatoes (red and yellow if available), halved
15 g/½ oz pine nuts, toasted

Yogurt dressing:
75 ml/3 fl oz low-fat natural dairy or soya yoghurt*
1 tablespoon lemon or lime juice
1 teaspoon finely chopped mint
salt and pepper

Garlic croûtons:
3 slices day-old ciabatta bread
1 garlic clove, peeled and left whole

■ Toss the spinach, lamb's lettuce and mint leaves together and place in a salad bowl or serving platter. Scatter the cherry tomatoes and pine nuts over the top.
■ Mix all the dressing ingredients together and season to taste. Drizzle over the salad leaves – serve any leftover dressing in a jug on the side.
■ To make the croûtons, toast both sides of the bread. Rub the clove of garlic over the surfaces and then cut into little cubes. Scatter over the salad just before serving.

Serves 4

PER SERVING
■
89 kcals (372 kj)
Protein 4 g
Fat 3 g
Carbohydrate 11 g
Fibre 1 g

VEGAN

THAI TOFU DIP

PER SERVING

■

45 kcals (185 kj)
Protein 3 g
Fat 3 g
Carbohydrate 2 g
Fibre 0.3

If you are buying a ready-made curry paste, make sure it is vegetarian as some contain fish sauce. If you prefer to make your own, use the recipe below.

100 g/4 oz silken tofu
1 teaspoon vegetable oil
1 small onion, finely chopped
1 tablespoon Thai green curry paste
2 tablespoons water

Green curry paste:
1 shallot, finely chopped
1 stalk lemon grass, chopped
2 small red chillies, chopped
2 garlic cloves, crushed
2.5-cm/1-in piece fresh root ginger, peeled and grated
grated zest of 1 lime
1 tablespoon chopped fresh coriander leaves and stalks

■ If making your own curry paste, grind all the ingredients in a pestle and mortar until you have a paste. (This will make more than you need. Store the excess in a screwtop jar in the refrigerator for up to 2 weeks.)
■ Drain the tofu and place in a blender or food processor.
■ Heat the oil and sauté the onion for 3 minutes. Add 1 tablespoon green curry paste and cook, stirring, for 2 minutes. Remove from the heat and cool.
■ Add to the tofu in the blender or food processor. Blend until smooth. Serve with a selection of raw vegetable crudités.

Serves 4

SUN-DRIED
TOMATO DIP

VEGAN

8 pieces of sun-dried tomato
1 garlic clove, crushed
grated zest and juice of 1 lemon
400-g/14-oz can of haricot beans,
   rinsed and drained
150 g/5 oz silken tofu
dash of Tabasco
salt and pepper
vegetable crudités, to serve

■ Soak the sun-dried tomatoes in boiling water to reconstitute. Drain, reserving the liquid.

■ Chop the tomatoes and place in a blender or food processor with the garlic, lemon zest and juice, beans and tofu. Blend to a dipping consistency, adding a little of the soaking water if required.

■ Season with Tabasco and salt and pepper to taste and serve with vegetable crudités.

Serves 6

PER SERVING

■

145 kcals (601 kJ)
Protein 7 g
Fat 8 g
Carbohydrate 13 g
Fibre 4 g

TERIYAKI DRESSING

Teriyaki sauce is a ready-made marinade mixture, including shoyu, ginger, garlic, and honey among its ingredients. It makes an excellent basis for a salad dressing as well as for marinades.

2 tablespoons teryaki sauce
1 tablespoon rice vinegar
1 teaspoon sesame oil
1 teaspoon honey
1 tablespoon chopped fresh coriander
salt and pepper

■ Mix all the ingredients together and serve with a beansprout salad or a salad of exotic mushrooms. (It can also be used to marinate vegetables before grilling or cooking over hot coals on a barbecue.)

Serves 4

PER SERVING

■

28 kcals (117 kJ)
Protein 0.6 g
Fat 1 g
Carbohydrate 4 g
Added sugar 3 g

VEGAN

PER SERVING
■
42 kcals (180 kj)
Protein 1 g
Fat 0.5 g
Carbohydrates 9 g
Added sugar 2 g
Fibre 1 g

SWEETCORN SALSA

A salsa is a cross between a dressing, a sauce and a salad – more of a relish. Wonderful served with salads, spicy foods and 'burgers', this recipe is very low in fat.

100 g/4 oz canned or frozen
  sweetcorn
25 g/1 oz onion, chopped
100 g/4 oz tomatoes, skinned and
  chopped
¼ cucumber, chopped
50 g/2 oz radish, sliced

1 red chilli, deseeded and finely
  chopped
15 g/½ oz fresh coriander or basil,
  chopped
juice of 1 lime
salt

■ If using frozen sweetcorn, cook according to the packet instructions and then cool.
■ Mix all the ingredients together and add a little salt to taste.
■ Leave the salsa to stand at room temperature, covered, for 1 hour before serving.

Serves 4

VEGAN

PER SERVING
■
32 kcals (137 kj)
Protein 1 g
Fat 0.1 g
Carbohydrate 7 g
Fibre 1 g

CUCUMBER, APPLE, ONION AND MINT RELISH

This relish is a good accompaniment for curries, cheese and salads and is very low in fat.

½ cucumber
2 dessert apples
1 small onion, chopped

1 tablespoon chopped mint
pinch of salt
1 tablespoon white wine vinegar

■ Cut the cucumber into quarters lengthways. Cut each long piece into 5-mm/¼-in chunks. Core the apples and cut into small cubes.
■ Mix all the ingredients together in a bowl and serve.

Serves 4

Opposite: Sweetcorn salsa and Cucumber, apple, onion and mint relish

VEGAN

BANANA, ONION
AND TOMATO CHUTNEY

This is a fresh chutney rather than a chutney for storing. Make just before serving as the banana can discolour and soften quickly.

1 banana, chopped
225 g/8 oz tomatoes, skinned and
   chopped
¼ red onion, finely chopped

15 g/½ oz fresh coriander chopped
juice of ½ lemon
salt
fresh coriander leaves, to garnish

■ Mix all the ingredients together in a bowl.
■ Garnish with coriander leaves and serve with Vegetable and Black Eye Bean Bangalore (see page 66) or Enchilladas with black bean and sweetcorn filling (see page 71) or other spicy dish of your choice.

Serves 4

PER SERVING
■
36 kcals (150 kj)
Protein 1 g
Fat 0.3 g
Carbohydrate 8 g
Fibre 1 g

VEGAN

FRESH ORANGE
AND DATE CHUTNEY

This is one of my favourite chutneys. We use it on the Cordon Vert diploma course as part of an Indian banquet.

225 g/8 oz stoned dates, coarsely
   chopped
2 oranges, peeled and segmented
juice of ½ lemon
3 tablespoons cider vinegar
120 ml/4 fl oz water
1 tablespoon maple syrup

2.5-cm/1-in piece fresh ginger root,
   peeled and thinly sliced
1 teaspoon yellow mustard seeds
1 teaspoon ground allspice or
   cinnamon
pinch of cayenne pepper
pinch of salt

■ Put all the ingredients into a saucepan and cook together over a low heat for about 45 minutes until soft . Cool.
■ Pour into a sterilized jar and seal. This chutney will keep for several weeks if refrigerated in a sealed container.

Serves 6

PER SERVING
■
134 kcals (569 kj)
Protein 2 g
Fat 0.4 g
Carbohydrate 32.5 g
Fibre 2 g

COURGETTE RELISH

VEGAN

I use up the glut of courgettes from the garden each year making this relish. It will keep in an airtight container in the refrigerator for up to three days.

1 tablespoon olive oil
225 g/8 oz courgettes, diced
1 small onion, chopped
¼ red pepper, very finely sliced
1 red chilli, very finely chopped

1 teaspoon yellow mustard seeds
3 tablespoons red wine vinegar
2 teaspoons light muscovado sugar
pinch of mustard powder
salt

■ Heat the oil and gently cook the courgettes, onion, red pepper, chilli and mustard seeds for 5 minutes.

■ Add the vinegar, sugar and mustard powder, mix well and continue to cook, stirring, for a further 5–10 minutes until the vegetables are tender and most of the liquid has evaporated. Season to taste

■ Cool, chill in the refrigerator and serve with Mushroom, Pepper and Tomato Stew (see page 67).

Serves 4

PER SERVING
■
58 kcals (240 kj)
Protein 2 g
Fat 3 g
Carbohydrate 5.5 g
Fibre 1 g

ONION MARMALADE

VEGAN

This 'marmalade' can be used as a relish to serve with dishes such as Wild Mushroom Risotto (see page 64) or Bubble and Squeak Patties (see page 58). It is also delicious scattered over a simple green salad with a squeeze of lemon juice.

1 tablespoon olive oil
2 red onions, sliced
1 tablespoon light muscovado sugar

150 ml/¼ pint wine
salt and pepper

■ Heat the oil in a frying pan and sweat the onions over a low heat until starting to brown. Add the sugar, cover and cook gently for about 10 minutes until caramelized.

■ Remove the lid, add the wine and cook until the liquid has almost disappeared. Season to taste and serve as a relish with savoury dishes.

Serves 4

PER SERVING
■
78 kcals (325 kj)
Protein 0.4 g
Fat 3 g
Carbohydrates 7.5 g
Fibre 0.4 g

DESSERTS

Strawberries with black pepper
Lemon grass sorbet
Plum and cherry summer pudding
Peach and pear compote with cinnamon
Strawberry mousse
Mango and orange fool
Orange, almond and cinnamon biscuits
Tofu cheesecake
Brandied apricot stacks
Apple and blackberry filo pie
Fruity topping
Rice pudding
Apple and date cake
Stuffed pears with ginger custard
Apple, orange and raspberry nutty crumble

Left: Brandied apricot stacks (page 114)

STRAWBERRIES
WITH BLACK PEPPER

This rather unlikely combination is very refreshing served with the Lemon Grass Sorbet below.

450 g/1 lb ripe English strawberries
1 tablespoon balsamic vinegar
1 teaspoon freshly ground black pepper

mint leaves and black pepper, to serve

■ Wash and halve the strawberries and place in a ceramic dish. Sprinkle over the balsamic vinegar and black pepper and toss gently.
■ Cover with clingfilm and leave to marinate for at least 30–60 minutes.
■ Serve decorated with mint leaves and a sprinkling of black pepper.

Serves 4

LEMON GRASS SORBET

This has the most refreshing, light flavour of any sorbet, perfect at the end of a richly flavoured meal.

175 g/6 oz caster sugar
300 ml/½ pint water

4 stalks lemon grass, cut into 2.5-cm/1-in lengths
juice of 3 lemons

■ Dissolve the sugar in the water in a saucepan over a low heat, stirring until thoroughly dissolved. Bruise the lemon grass with a rolling pin and add to the saucepan. Boil for 3–4 minutes to make a sugar syrup.
■ Remove from the heat and leave to infuse for 1 hour. Strain through a fine sieve and stir in the lemon juice. Pour into a polythene container and freeze, uncovered, until half-frozen. Mash the mixture well and freeze until solid.
■ Remove the sorbet from the freezer 10–20 minutes before serving. Mash with a fork to break up the ice crystals, then shape between 2 serving spoons.

Serves 6

PEAR SORBET VARIATION
■

Peel, core and stew 675 g/ 1½ lb pears. Purée the pears; boil the stewing liquid until reduced to 300 ml/½ pint. Mix together and freeze as for the Lemon Grass Sorbet.

Opposite: Lemon grass sorbet with Strawberries with black pepper

PLUM AND CHERRY
SUMMER PUDDING

This is an autumnal variation on an old favourite which is usually made with summer berries. If you can't get fresh fruit, use canned fruit in natural juice; if the fruit is in syrup, reduce the amount of caster sugar added.

450 g/1 lb plums, stoned
450 g/1 lb cherries, stoned
100 g/4 oz caster sugar
10 slices white bread, crusts removed
cherry pairs on stalks, to decorate

■ Place the fruit in a saucepan with the sugar and 2 tablespoons water. Cover and cook over a gentle heat until soft. Cool and drain, reserving the juice.
■ Cut out a circle of bread to fit the base of a 900-ml/1½-pint pudding basin. Cut the remaining bread into 2.5-cm/1-in wide strips.
■ Dip the bread into the reserved juice and use to line the pudding basin, overlapping the strips.
■ Spoon the fruit into the lined basin and add any remaining juice. Cover with the remaining bread.
■ Place a small plate on top of the bread. Put a weight on top and refrigerate overnight.
■ Turn out the summer pudding onto a serving plate and decorate with pairs of cherries.

Serves 6

PER SERVING

■

188 kcals (791 kj)
Protein 3 g
Fat 0.5 g
Carbohydrate 45 g
Fibre 2 g

PEACH AND PEAR
COMPOTE WITH CINNAMON

100 g/4 oz dried pears
100 g/4 oz dried peaches
5-cm/2-in piece of cinnamon stick
150 ml/¼ pint red wine

150 ml/¼ pint water
1 apple and cinnamon tea bag
  (optional)

■ Place the dried pears and peaches in a saucepan with the cinnamon stick. Mix the wine and water together and pour over the dried fruit. Add the tea bag, if using, and leave to soak for 1–2 hours.
■ Place the pan over a gentle heat and cook the fruit for about 30 minutes until soft.
■ Serve hot or cold with Pear Sorbet (see page 106).

Serves 4

STRAWBERRY MOUSSE

If you use English strawberries in season, you should not need to add any sugar to this colourful dessert. Children will love it.

225 g/8 oz silken tofu
450 g/1 lb ripe strawberries, washed
  and dried
grated zest of 1 orange

2 tablespoons crème de cassis
  (optional)
15 g/½ oz icing sugar (optional)

■ Drain the tofu and place in a blender or food processor.
■ Reserve 4 strawberries with the calyx intact. Roughly chop the rest and add to the blender or food processor with the orange zest and crème de cassis (if using).
■ Blend well until smooth, and then spoon into sundae glasses and chill in the refrigerator.
■ Slice through the reserved strawberries upwards from the base, leaving the top and calyx intact, and fan them out. Decorate each chilled mousse with a fanned strawberry and serve with Orange, Almond and Cinnamon Biscuits (see page 112).

Serves 4

Mango and
ORANGE FOOL

To reduce the fat content in this dessert you could leave out the soya cream from the recipe, but for a special treat, the extra creaminess is welcome.

PER SERVING

■

201 kcals (836 kj)
Protein 7 g
Fat 11 g
Carbohydrate 19 g
Fibre 3.5 g

225 g/8 oz silken tofu
150 ml/¼ pint soya cream
5-cm/2-in piece fresh root ginger, peeled and grated
2 ripe mangoes
1 orange
2 tablespoons caster sugar
1 teaspoon vanilla essence

■ Drain the tofu and place in a blender with the soya cream and grated ginger. Peel and stone 1 mango and roughly chop the flesh. Add to the blender.
■ Zest the orange and reserve some of the strips for decoration. Put the remaining zest in the blender with the sugar and vanilla essence. Blend until smooth.
■ Peel, stone and cube the remaining mango. Segment the orange and chop each segment into 3. Mix together.
■ Divide half of the tofu mixture between 4 sundae glasses. Layer the fruit on top and cover with the remaining tofu mixture. Chill in the refrigerator.
■ Decorate with the reserved orange zest and serve with Orange, Almond and Cinnamon Biscuits (see page 112).

Serves 4

Opposite: Mango and orange fool with
Orange, almond and cinnamon biscuits (page 112)

VEGAN

ORANGE, ALMOND
AND CINNAMON BISCUITS

Although these biscuits contain quite a lot of fat, they are delicious served with a low-fat dessert such as Strawberry Mousse (see page 109) to add a little 'crunch'.

PER SERVING
■

132 kcals (550 kj)
Protein 2 g
Fat 9 g
Carbohydrate 11 g
Fibre 1 g

---

50 g/2 oz self-raising flour
50 g/2 oz ground almonds
25 g/1 oz porridge oats
25 g/1 oz demerara sugar
1 teaspoon ground cinnamon
grated zest and juice of 1 orange
50 g/2 oz soft vegan margarine
1 teaspoon orange essence

■ Preheat the oven to 180°C/350°F/Gas Mark 4.

■ Mix the flour, ground almonds and porridge oats together in a large bowl. Add the sugar, cinnamon and orange zest and mix well.

■ Melt the margarine in a saucepan together with the orange juice. Stir into the dry ingredients together with the orange essence. Mix to form a smooth dough, adding a little more orange juice if necessary.

■ Turn out onto a lightly floured surface and roll out to about 5 mm/¼ inch thick. Use a 5-cm/2-in pastry cutter to make 12 biscuits. Place on a greased baking sheet and bake in the preheated oven for 20–30 minutes.

■ Cool on a wire rack and serve with the dessert of your choice.

Makes 8 biscuits

TOFU CHEESECAKE

Tofu makes an excellent substitute for cream cheese in this dessert, reducing the fat level considerably.

175 g/6 oz vegan ginger biscuits
50 g/2 oz vegan margarine

Topping:
300 g/10 oz silken tofu, drained
1 tablespoon maple syrup
225 g/8 oz raspberries (defrost if using frozen)
3 tablespoons agar agar flakes
150 ml/¼ pint water

To decorate:
15 g/½ oz toasted desiccated coconut
extra raspberries and sprigs of mint

PER SERVING
■
194 kcals (810 kj)
Protein 4 g
Fat 12 g
Carbohydrates 18 g
Added sugar 1 g
Fibre 3 g

■ Crush the ginger biscuits with a rolling pin to make fine crumbs.

■ Melt the margarine in a saucepan and stir in the crumbs. Press immediately into a 17-cm/7-in spring-mould tin. Chill in the refrigerator.

■ Put the silken tofu and maple syrup in a blender or food processor.

■ Push the raspberries through a plastic sieve to remove the pips and add the pulp to the blender or food processor. Blend until smooth.

■ Place the agar agar and water in a small saucepan. Bring to the boil, stirring all the time, then reduce the heat and simmer until dissolved. Add to the blender or processor and blend again.

■ Pour over the chilled crumb base and leave to set in the refrigerator for at least 2 hours.

■ Turn out the cheesecake onto a serving plate. Sprinkle the toasted coconut round the top edge and decorate with raspberries and sprigs of mint.

Serves 8

BRANDIED
APRICOT STACKS

An elegant dish for a dinner party, this dessert uses filo pastry which has a lower fat content than puff or shortcrust pastry.

PER SERVING

■

260 kcals (1085 kj)
Protein 7 g
Fat 7 g
Carbohydrates 45 g
Added sugar 0.6 g
Fibre 2 g

100 g/4 oz filo pastry
15 g/½ oz vegan margarine, melted
100 g/4 oz dried apricots, finely chopped
2 tablespoons brandy
600 ml/1 pint cold thick custard (made with soya milk)

To decorate:
icing sugar, for dusting
sprigs of mint

■ Preheat the oven to 200°C/400°F/Gas Mark 6.
■ Take 3 sheets of filo pastry at a time, and brush each layer with a little melted margarine. Lay the sheets on top of each other. Use a pastry cutter to cut into 7.5-cm/3-in disks. You will need 12 altogether.
■ Brush the top of each disk with a little melted margarine and place on a baking sheet lined with baking parchment. Cover with another sheet of baking parchment and another baking sheet. Place an ovenproof dish on top to weigh it down and bake in the preheated oven for 10–15 minutes until cooked. Cool.
■ Soak the apricots in brandy for 30 minutes, and then stir into the cold custard.
■ Place one disk of filo on each of 4 serving plates. Spoon the apricot custard on top. Repeat with another layer of each and top with a filo disk. Sift a little icing sugar over the stack, decorate with mint sprigs and serve.

Serves 6

Note: You may want to make a few extra disks of filo pastry to allow for breakages as they are quite fragile.

Opposite: Brandied apricot stacks

Apple and BLACKBERRY FILO PIE

Blackberries are a good source of vitamin C. If you are picking your own, choose a site well away from the roadside.

450 g/1 lb cooking apples, peeled, cored and sliced
225 g/8 oz blackberries, washed
50 g/2 oz sugar

1 teaspoon mixed spice (optional)
3 sheets filo pastry
15 g/½ oz vegan margarine, melted
25 /1 oz flaked almonds

■ Preheat the oven to 190°C/375°F/Gas Mark 5.
■ Stew the apples gently in a little water for about 10 minutes until nearly cooked.
■ Allow to cool, then layer the apples and blackberries in a pie dish and sprinkle over the sugar and mixed spice (if using).
■ Brush one sheet of filo with melted margarine and place over the filling. Trim to fit. Repeat with the remaining 2 sheets.
■ Sprinkle the flaked almonds over the top and bake in the preheated oven for 20–30 minutes until golden.

Serves 4

FRUITY TOPPING

Serve this delicious low-fat topping with desserts in place of cream or soya cream.

225 g/8 oz silken tofu, drained
juice and grated zest of 1 orange
½ teaspoon orange essence

1 teaspoon lemon juice
1 tablespoon Cointreau (optional)

■ Blend all the ingredients together in a blender. Cover and chill in the refrigerator until needed.
■ Use as a vegan substitute for cream on fruity desserts.

Serves 8

Opposite: Apple and blackberry filo pie

RICE PUDDING

This traditional pudding is high in carbohydrate and vitamins. You can vary the fresh fruit according to what is in season.

PER SERVING
■

117 kcals (492 kj)
Protein 4 g
Fat 0.4 g
Carbohydrate 25 g
Fibre 1 g

50 g/2 oz flaked rice
600 ml/1 pint skimmed milk or soya
  milk*
25 g/1 oz raw sugar
50 g/2 oz sultanas

½ teaspoon ground nutmeg or
  cinnamon
1 apple, cored and sliced
1 orange, peeled and segmented
1 peach, stoned and sliced

■ Place the flaked rice, milk, sugar, sultanas and spices in a saucepan. Bring to the boil, then reduce the heat and gently simmer, covered, for about 15 minutes until the rice is soft. Stir frequently to prevent sticking.

■ Spoon the rice pudding into a serving dish and decorate with the fresh fruit. Serve immediately.

Serves 6

APPLE AND DATE CAKE

There is no added sugar in this cake. The sweetness comes from the fruit itself.

PER SERVING
■

217 kcals (913 kj)
Protein 6 g
Fat 8 g
Carbohydrate 33 g
Fibre 2 g

225 g/8 oz self-raising flour
1 teaspoon ground cinnamon
1 tablespoon lemon juice
150 ml/5 fl oz low-fat natural yogurt
2 free-range eggs, beaten

100 ml/4 fl oz vegetable oil
225 g/8 oz Bramley apples, peeled,
  cored and diced
100 g/4 oz chopped dates

■ Preheat the oven to 180°C/350°F/Gas Mark 4. Grease and line a deep 20-cm/8-in cake tin with baking parchment.

■ Sift the flour and cinnamon into a large mixing bowl. Beat the lemon juice, yogurt, eggs and oil together and add to the flour. Beat well to combine. Stir in the apples and dates and spoon into the prepared cake tin.

■ Bake in the preheated oven for about 1¼ hours until risen and golden brown. Allow to cool for 5 minutes in the tin and then turn out onto a wire cooling rack.

■ Serve cold with low-fat fromage frais or soya cream, if liked.

Serves 8

STUFFED PEARS
WITH GINGER CUSTARD

A wintry combination of pears, ginger and custard makes this dessert, which is high in carbohydrate, very more-ish! It has a tantalisingly festive smell, reminiscent of Christmas, when cooking.

4 large pears, peeled and cored
50 g/2 oz dried mixed fruit
1 piece stem ginger in syrup, finely chopped
2 tablespoons syrup from the ginger
4 tablespoons vegan custard powder*
25 g/1 oz caster sugar
1 teaspoon ground ginger
600 ml/1 pint skimmed milk or soya milk*

PER SERVING
■
228 kcals (962 kj)
Protein 6 g
Fat 0.5 g
Carbohydrate 53 g
Fibre 3 g

■ Preheat the oven to 190°C/375°F/Gas Mark 5.
■ Place the pears in an ovenproof dish.
■ Mix the dried fruit, ginger and syrup together and use to fill the cavities in the pears. Put 4 tablespoons water in the dish, cover with foil and bake in the preheated oven for 40–45 minutes until tender.
■ Mix the custard powder*, sugar and ground ginger together with a little of the milk. Heat the remaining milk in a saucepan. Pour over the custard powder, mix well then return to the pan and simmer for 3 minutes, stirring all the time, until thick. Serve with the stuffed pears.

Serves 4

APPLE, ORANGE
AND RASPBERRY NUTTY CRUMBLE

PER SERVING
■
269 kcals (1120 kj)
Protein 6 g
Fat 17 g
Carbohydrate 25 g
Fibre 4 g

It is difficult to make a dish involving nuts low in fat! This recipe relies on almonds and muesli to give the crunch to the crumble topping and these ingredients are good source of protein for vegetarians, so sometimes one has to be weighed against the other.

100 g/4 oz ground almonds
50 g/2 oz muesli
50 g/2 oz vegan margarine
25 g/1 oz demerara sugar
soya cream or ice cream, to serve

Fruit filling:
225 g/8 oz cooking apples, peeled, cored and sliced
2 oranges, peeled and all pith removed
225 g/8 oz raspberries (frozen)
25 g/1 oz caster sugar

■ Preheat the oven to 180°C/350°F/Gas Mark 4.
■ To make the nutty topping, mix the ground almonds and muesli together in a bowl. Rub in the vegan margarine and stir in the sugar.
■ Layer the apples in an ovenproof dish. Cut the oranges across the grain to make circles and place on top of the apples. Top with the raspberries and sprinkle over the sugar.
■ Spoon the nutty topping evenly over the fruit and bake in the preheated oven for 40–50 minutes. Serve hot with soya cream or ice cream.

Serves 6

Opposite: Apple, orange and raspberry nutty crumble

SNACKS,
SANDWICHES
AND DRINKS

Chilli tamari seeds
Smoked tofu and tomatoes on grilled ciabatta
Cheesy mushroom scramble on toasted
  baguette
Filled bagels
Pitta pockets with hummus and sprouted
  beans
Pitta pockets with rocket and tabbouleh salad
Pitta pockets with falafels
Tortilla wrap with bean and salsa filling
Bruschetta
Jacket potatoes with healthy toppings
Strawberry smoothie drink
Tropical drink

Left: Tortilla wrap with bean and salsa filling (page 130)

CHILLI TAMARI SEEDS

Serve these nutritious nibbles with drinks before a meal. Pumpkin seeds are an excellent source of zinc.

25 g/1 oz pumpkin seeds   ½–1 teaspoon chilli powder
25 g/1 oz sunflower seeds   1–2 tablespoons tamari

■ Place the seeds in a heavy-based pan without any oil. Toast over a high flame, shaking the pan to ensure that the seeds are evenly toasted. (You may want to put a lid on the pan as the seeds tend to crack and jump.)
■ When the seeds are golden, remove from the heat and add the chilli powder. Shake or stir to coat.
■ When the pan has cooled a little, add the tamari and stir well to coat.
■ Serve as a nibble with drinks or use to scatter over plain green salads.

Serves 6

SMOKED TOFU
AND TOMATOES ON GRILLED CIABATTA

8 slices day-old ciabatta bread   25 g/1 oz stoned olives
225 g/8 oz packet smoked tofu   15 g/½ oz parsley, chopped
400-g/14-oz can of chopped   freshly ground black pepper
    tomatoes, drained

■ Preheat the grill. Toast the ciabatta bread slices on both sides and keep warm.
■ Slice the tofu into 'rashers' and grill gently on both sides for a couple of minutes until starting to colour. Cool a little and roughly chop.
■ Place the drained tomatoes in a saucepan and heat through gently.
■ Rinse the olives and drain well. Chop and add to the tomatoes together with the chopped tofu. Stir well to mix and heat through.
■ Pile on top of the warm toast. Sprinkle with chopped parsley and coarsely ground black pepper. Serve immediately.

Serves 4

CHEESY MUSHROOM
SCRAMBLE ON
TOASTED BAGUETTE

This high protein, energy giving snack is a wonderful lunchtime treat on a cold winter's day.

1 small baguette or ½ French stick
4 tomatoes, halved
30 ml/2 fl oz skimmed milk
50 g/2 oz low-fat vegetarian
   Cheddar cheese, grated
6 free-range eggs, lightly beaten
salt and freshly ground black pepper
15 g/½ oz butter
50 g/2 oz button mushrooms, sliced
snipped chives, to garnish

PER SERVING
■
325 kcals (1364 kj)
Protein 20 g
Fat 16 g
Carbohydrate 27 g
Fibre 1 g

■ Preheat the grill. Cut the baguette in half, then cut each piece in half along its length (as though making a sandwich). You should now have 4 long pieces of bread.

■ Toast under the preheated grill until golden. At the same time, grill the tomatoes.

■ Add the skimmed milk and grated cheese to the eggs and beat with a fork to combine. Season with a little salt and pepper.

■ Heat the butter in a large non-stick saucepan. Sauté the mushrooms for about 5 minutes until tender.

■ Pour the egg and cheese mixture into the pan. Stir continuously with a wooden spoon over a low heat until the softly scrambled egg forms. Remove from the heat and continue stirring until it reaches the required consistency.

■ Place the toasted baguettes on serving plates. Top each piece with the cheesy mushroom scramble. Garnish with the grilled tomatoes and sprinkle with snipped chives. Serve immediately.

Serves 4

FILLED BAGELS

SUN-DRIED TOMATO AND BASIL SPREAD

PER SERVING
■
145 kcals (613 kj)
Protein 6 g
Fat 3 g
Carbohydrate 25 g
Fibre 1 g

zest and juice of ½ lemon
3 tablespoons sun-dried tomato purée
1 tablespoon ground almonds
15 g/½ oz basil leaves
salt and freshly ground black pepper
4 bagels, split and toasted

■ Mix the lemon zest and juice with the tomato purée and ground almonds to form a thick paste.
■ Chop half of the basil and stir in. Season with salt and pepper to taste.
■ Spread on the toasted bagels and scatter the remaining basil leaves over the top.

Serves 4

QUARK AND AVOCADO TOPPING

PER SERVING
■
185 kcals (782 kj)
Protein 12.5 g
Fat 4 g
Carbohydrate 27 g
Fibre 2 g

200 g/7 oz quark
½ avocado, peeled, stoned and
    chopped
juice of ½ lemon
12 cherry tomatoes, quartered
15 g/½ oz fresh coriander or parsley,
    chopped
salt and freshly ground black pepper
4 bagels, split and toasted

■ Mix the quark with the chopped avocado, lemon juice, cherry tomatoes and herbs. Season with salt and pepper, and use to top the toasted bagel slices.

Serves 4

Opposite: Filled bagels with Sun-dried tomato and basil spread and Quark and avocado topping

VEGAN

PITTA POCKETS
WITH HUMMUS AND SPROUTED BEANS

400-g/14-oz can chick peas, rinsed and drained
2–3 tablespoons water
2 tablespoons tahini
juice of 1 lemon

1 tablespoon olive oil
2 garlic cloves, crushed
salt and pepper
4 pitta breads
100 g/4 oz mixed sprouted beans

■ Place the chick peas, water, tahini, lemon juice, olive oil and garlic in a food processor. Process until a rough pâté is achieved, adding more water if necessary. Season to taste.
■ Split the pitta breads down one side to make each into a pouch. Spread the hummus thickly inside and fill with sprouted beans.

Serves 4

VEGAN

PITTA POCKETS
WITH ROCKET AND TABBOULEH SALAD

4 pitta breads
50 g/2 oz rocket leaves
50 g/2 oz endive
150 g/5 oz Mixed Grain Tabbouleh Salad (see page 82)
salad dressing of your choice

■ Split the pitta breads down one side to make each into a pouch.
■ Line each pitta bread with a mixture of rocket and endive leaves. Pile about 2 tablespoons of tabbouleh into each pocket and drizzle the salad dressing of your choice over.

Serves 4

PITTA POCKETS
WITH FALAFELS

400-g/14-oz can chick peas, rinsed and drained
75 g/3 oz onion, very finely diced
2 tablespoons finely chopped parsley
2 tablespoons finely chopped mint
2 garlic cloves, crushed
2 teaspoons ground coriander
2 teaspoons ground cumin
pinch of chilli powder
1 tablespoon gram flour mixed to a paste with 2 tablespoons water
salt and pepper
25 g/1 oz unbleached white flour
4 wholemeal pitta breads
50 g/2 oz mixed salad leaves

For the dressing:
150 ml/5 fl oz natural soya yogurt
1 tablespoon finely chopped mint
1 tablespoon lemon juice
salt to taste

PER SERVING
■
460 kcals (1953 kj)
Protein 21 g
Fat 7 g
Carbohydrate 84 g
Fibre 8 g

■ Preheat the oven to 190°C/375°F/Gas Mark 5. Lightly grease a baking sheet.
■ Grind the chick peas in a nut grinder or blender and transfer to a large bowl. Add the onion, parsley, mint, garlic and spices and mix well. Bind with the gram flour paste and season with salt and pepper.
■ Form the mixture into balls about the size of a walnut (it should make 12–16). Coat very lightly with unbleached flour, place on the greased baking sheet and cook in the preheated oven for about 20–25 minutes until golden, turning once.
■ Make the dressing by mixing the yogurt, mint and lemon juice together. Season to taste with salt.
■ Halve the pitta breads to make each into 2 small pockets. Chop the salad leaves roughly and fill each half. Push 2 falafels into each half and drizzle the dressing over. Serve immediately.

Serves 4

TORTILLA WRAP WITH
BEAN AND SALSA FILLING

Refried beans are pinto beans. If you can't buy them canned, use kidney beans and mash them lightly with a potato masher.

8 large soft flour tortillas
400-g/14-oz can of refried beans
1 quantity Tomato Salsa (see page 132)
4 spring onions, shredded

¼ cucumber, sliced
½ avocado, peeled, stoned and chopped
8 iceberg lettuce leaves, shredded

∎ Preheat the oven to 190°C/375°F/Gas Mark 5.
∎ Wrap the tortillas in foil and warm in the preheated oven for 5–10 minutes.
∎ Meanwhile, place the refried beans in a bowl and add the salsa, spring onions, cucumber and avocado and mix well.
∎ Place shredded lettuce on each tortilla. Top with the bean and salsa mixture. Fold each tortilla in half over the filling and roll up. Cut in half and serve.

Makes 8

BRUSCHETTA

Once fashionable, but now accepted as almost traditional on many menus, bruschetta make an excellent snack.

1 ciabatta loaf, cut into 12 slices
2 tablespoons vegan pesto
4 ripe tomatoes, skinned and roughly chopped

15 g/½ oz basil leaves, roughly torn
4 teaspoons balsamic vinegar
freshly ground black pepper

∎ Preheat the grill and toast the ciabatta slices on both sides.
∎ Spread a little vegan pesto on each slice. Top with tomato and basil leaves.
∎ Drizzle the balsamic vinegar over the topping and grind some black pepper on top. Serve immediately.

Serves 4

Opposite: Tortilla wrap with bean and salsa filling

Jacket potatoes
with HEALTHY TOPPINGS

**PER AVERAGE
POTATO**
■

245 kcals (1024 kj)
Protein 7 g
Fat 0.4 g
Carbohydrate 57 g
Fibre 5 g

4 large baking potatoes

Tahini and chive topping*:
juice of ½ lemon
3 tablespoons tahini
½ teaspoon yeast extract, dissolved
   in a little water
3 tablespoons water
15 g/½ oz chives, chopped
salt and pepper

**Low fat fromage frais
with herbs:**
200 g/7 oz low-fat fromage frais
handful of fresh herbs, e.g. basil and
   parsley, chopped
salt and pepper

Tomato salsa*:
225 g/8 oz ripe tomatoes, skinned
   and chopped
¼ red onion, finely chopped
15 g/½ oz fresh coriander, finely
   chopped
salt and pepper

Apple and hazelnut coleslaw*:
1 dessert apple, peeled and grated
50 g/2 oz cabbage, finely shredded
1 shallot, chopped
15 g/½ oz chopped roast hazelnuts
2 tablespoons Tofu Mayonnaise (see
   page 90) or ready-made vegan
   mayonnaise
1 teaspoon hazelnut oil

■ Cook the baking potatoes in a preheated oven at 200°C/400°F/Gas Mark 6, for about 1–1½ hours until tender. Alternatively, cook in a microwave oven.
■ Mix all the ingredients of your chosen topping together thoroughly (use a blender or food processor for the tahini and chive topping). Serve with jacket potatoes.

Serves 4

Opposite: Jacket potatoes with healthy toppings

TAHINI TOPPING ■	**FROMAGE FRAIS TOPPING** ■	**SALSA TOPPING** ■	**COLESLAW TOPPING** ■
156 kcals (644 kj)	33 kcals (139 kj)	13 kcals (52 kj)	66 kcals (263 kj)
Protein 5 g	Protein 4 g	Protein 0.6 g	Protein 1 g
Fat 15 g	Fat 0.2 g	Fat 0.2 g	Fat 5 g
Carbohydrate 0.5 g	Carbohydrate 4 g	Carbohydrate 2 g	Carbohydrate 4 g
Fibre 2 g	Fibre 0.2 g	Fibre 0.6 g	Fibre 1 g

STRAWBERRY
SMOOTHIE DRINK

PER SERVING

■

130 kcals (546 kj)
Protein 8 g
Fat 1 g
Carbohydrate 23 g
Fibre 1.5 g

Strawberries are full of vitamin C and this is a very refreshing way of enjoying them. If you can buy English strawberries in season, you will find they are naturally sweeter than imported ones. If the drink is a little too tart for your taste, add a little icing sugar – but it won't be as healthy!

450 g/1 lb ripe strawberries, washed
1 banana
450 ml/15 fl oz low-fat natural
    yogurt

150 ml/¼ pint skimmed milk
1 teaspoon vanilla extract
6–8 ice cubes, crushed

■ Place the strawberries, banana, yogurt, milk and vanilla extract in a blender and blend until smooth.
■ Put the crushed ice into 4 tall glasses, pour the smoothie over the ice and serve immediately.

Serves 4

VEGAN

TROPICAL DRINK

PER SERVING

■

76 kcals (320 kj)
Protein 1 g
Fat 0.3 g
Carbohydrate 19 g
Fibre 1.5 g

600ml/1 pint pineapple juice, chilled
4 kiwi fruit, peeled and chopped
2 ripe mangoes, peeled, stoned and
    chopped

600 ml/1 pint soda water, chilled
6 ice cubes, crushed
sprigs of mint, to serve

■ Put the pineapple juice, kiwi fruit and mango flesh in a blender. Blend until smooth.
■ Pour into a large serving jug and chill in the refrigerator. Just before serving, add the soda water.
■ Place a little crushed ice in the bottom of each glass, pour over the drink and serve immediately.

Serves 6

Opposite: Tropical drink and Strawberry smoothie drink

MENU SUGGESTIONS

BREAKFASTS

Breakfast is the most important meal of the day. In literally breaking the fast that your body has been on while you have been sleeping, you boost your blood sugar and energy levels. Breakfasts tend to be high-carbohydrate meals in order to supply this energy, and it is a good rule to include a glass of orange juice or one or two pieces of fresh fruit to provide some of the vitamins that you need, especially vitamin C.

Here are some examples of balanced breakfasts that you can put together easily to give you a good start to the day:

MENU 1
- Fresh Fruit Salad with Granola and fromage frais or yogurt
- Savoury Muffin

High in carbohydrate and protein

MENU 2
- Creamed Mushrooms on Toast, using the Seed or Herb Bread for toast
- Fruit Crêpes

High in carbohydrates, B vitamins, potassium and iron.

MENU 3
- Granola with milk or soya milk
- Cinnamon and Raisin Bread, toasted if liked, with a little butter or vegan margarine

This is reasonably high in fat because of the nuts in the granola and milk but it is a good protein meal, containing nuts, seeds, grains and milk/soya milk; the dried fruit is a good source of iron.

MENU 4
- Grilled Honeyed Citrus Fruits
- Baked Beans in Tomato Sauce
- Seed Bread, toasted

High in vitamin C and carbohydrates, and low in fat.

MENU 5
A weekend breakfast that could form brunch!
- Healthy Hash Browns with Tomatoes and Rashers, or Tofu Kedgeree
- Baked Beans in Tomato Sauce
- Breakfast Muffins and low-sugar preserves

This is a slightly larger breakfast for a late weekend start which could form both breakfast and lunch. Add an apple to give you a raw ingredient (remember, five-a-day) and this should carry you through the day until your evening meal.

LUNCHES

The sort of food you choose for lunch often depends on your lifestyle. If you are out at work all day and don't have access to cooking facilities at lunchtime, then one of the sandwich-style recipes may suit you. If you are at home all day, you may have more time for something like a soup which you can make in advance and then warm through quite quickly. Here are some suggestions for balanced lunches to suit different lifestyles:

MENU 1

Packed lunch for children, teenagers or adults.

Pick one of the following recipes and combine it with one or two pieces of fruit:
- **Pitta Pockets with Hummus and Sprouted Beans**
- **Pitta Pockets with Falafels**
- **Pitta Pockets with Rocket and Tabbouleh Salad**

These three recipes are high in protein and carbohydrates, and the sprouted beans and salads are full of vitamins, too. The rocket salad may be more suitable for an adult, being slightly bitter in flavour, but you could substitute other salad leaves for a child.

- **Bagels with Quark and Avocado Topping**

One of the few dairy recipes, but quark is very low in fat so this is still a healthy option. Fresh herbs and tomatoes supply a raw element as well as vitamins.

- **Tortilla Wrap with Bean and Salsa Filling**

An interesting lunch suited to teenagers and adults. Avocados are a good source of EFAs and B group vitamins and with the salad ingredients this lunch is full of vitamins as well as protein and carbohydrate.

MENU 2

Lunches for weekends or for people with access to cooking facilities at lunchtime.

- **Jacket Potatoes with a variety of toppings**

Potatoes are a good source of starchy carbohydrate and vitamin C. Combine a jacket potato with the topping of your choice. The tomato salsa and fromage frais with herbs toppings are particularly low in fat.

- **Chickpea and Spinach Soup with Herb Bread**

Chickpeas are high in protein and minerals and spinach is a good source of iron and vitamin C. This low fat soup will keep you going during the day.

- **Pumpkin and Haricot Bean Soup with Seed Bread**

A hearty soup for colder days, which is high in carbohydrate.

MENU 3

Light lunches.

- **Minty Pea Dip with crudités**

A light summery lunch, which is generally high in vitamins, particularly vitamin C. Team this with a low-fat fruit yogurt for dessert to increase the protein.

- **Roast Pepper and Aubergine Mousse with Melba Toast**

Red peppers are high in beta-carotene and make this dip an appetising colour.

- **Fattoush with Lamb's Lettuce**

This is reasonably high in fat because of the cheese and egg, but you could reduce this by using tofu instead or leaving this element out altogether. Lots of salad so again a good source of vitamins and a great way of contributing to your 5-a-day.

MAIN MEALS

In many households, the main meal is served in the evening as one or more family members are out of the home during the day, often taking a packed lunch with them. If you are able to eat your main meal at lunchtime and have a lighter evening meal or supper, this will give your body more chance to burn up the calories before you rest at night. Substitute the lunch suggestions above for a light evening snack or perhaps the Malaysian Vermicelli or Roast Vegetable Tortillas for something light but substantial.

For main meals the following combinations are suggested:

MENU 1

Quick weekday meals when you are probably too busy to spend a long time in the kitchen – a main course dish and vegetable/salad accompaniments followed by fresh fruit or yogurt is probably sufficient

■ **Penne with Broccoli, Avocado and Roast Pepper**
Broccoli is sometimes called the ACE vegetable as it is high in vitamins A and C. The vitamin E in the avocado and pine nuts helps to protect these vitamins in the body.

■ **Asparagus Fettucine Stir-fry with Peanut Sauce, with Banana, Onion and Tomato Chutney**
Starchy pasta is a good source of carbohydrate and protein. The chutney provides vitamins, too, and the bananas are particularly high in potassium which helps to regulate the body's fluids. This meal is low in fat.

■ **Szechuan Tofu with rice and Japanese Sea Vegetable Salad**
A very tasty and quickly prepared mid-week meal. The rice, tofu and cashew nuts provide a good source of protein, but if you want to reduce the fat further either reduce the amount of cashew nuts or remove completely. The salad is very low in fat, and the sea

vegetables provide minerals and trace elements while the fresh vegetables are good for vitamins.

MENU 2

Low-calorie main meals

■ **Vegetable and Black Eye Bean Bangalore**
Although filling, this delicious curry is low in calories, but contains fresh fruit and vegetables to provide vitamins, and black eye beans for protein.

■ **Teryaki Stir-fry with Noodles and Sprouting Bean Salad with Ginger Dressing**
An oriental-style meal which is high in flavours but low in calories. The noodles provide protein while stir-frying the vegetables uses only a little fat and minimizes nutrient (vitamin) loss from the vegetables.

For low-calorie desserts try:
■ Strawberry Mousse
■ Lemon Grass Sorbet

MENU 3

Low-fat main meals

■ **Farfalle with Mange Tout, Flageolet Beans, Courgettes and Mint**
You could serve this with a green salad dressed with lemon juice in place of the garlic bread, if liked, but it will also stand on its own and is both tasty and nutritious. The pasta and cheese provide protein and the vegetables are a good source of vitamins.

■ **Millet Pilaf with Spicy Bean Salad**
This is low in fat but good for protein and carbohydrate with a wide range of vegetables and pulses for vitamins, too. Quite a hearty meal, good for winter.

For low-fat desserts try:
■ Rice Pudding
■ Plum and Cherry Summer Pudding

MENU 4

Teenager's menu

■ Potato Pizza with Mixed Pepper and Mushroom Topping
■ Strawberry Mousse

Obviously you can change the pizza topping, but the base is a good source of carbohydrate and protein while the topping with the range of vegetables is full of vitamins. The recipes provide a reasonable level of fat and of calories to provide fuel for active teenagers.

■ Bubble and Squeak Patties served with steamed vegetables or Mixed Green Salad with Tofu and Mango
■ Apple and Blackberry Filo Pie

These healthy oven-baked patties or burgers are great for a main meal. Teenagers need lots of calcium so introducing tofu, which often has a high-calcium but low-fat content, can be a good way of achieving this. The pie is filling, but not too high in calories, while providing fruit to increase vitamin intake.

MENU 5

High-protein menu

One of the questions frequently asked is 'Will I get enough protein on a vegetarian diet?'. There really is no problem with this as you will see from the analysis of the recipes. However, if you need a high-protein diet for a particular reason try some of the following.

For high-protein starters or light meals:
■ Pumpkin and Haricot Bean Soup
■ Tuscan Tomato Soup
■ Broad Bean, Lemon and Sage Dip
■ Caponata Crostini

For high-protein main dishes:
■ Farfalle with Mange Tout, Flageolet Beans, Courgettes and Mint
■ Broad Bean and Sweetcorn Stew
■ Marinated Tofu and Vegetable Filo Pie

Serve any of the above with steamed vegetables or salad of your choice for all-round balance.

For high protein desserts:
■ Apple, Orange and Raspberry Nutty Crumble
■ Stuffed Pears with Ginger Custard

MENU SUGGESTIONS FOR HEALTHY ENTERTAINING WITHOUT MISSING OUT!

For some reason it seems to be generally thought that if you are eating 'healthy' food or vegetarian food, you must be missing out on the treats. Combine the words 'healthy', 'vegetarian' and 'food' and most omnivores will think you wear a hair shirt, too! Prove to your guests that food that is good for you can be enjoyable and vice versa, with the following menu suggestions:

MENU 1

Far Eastern Evening:
■ Chinese-style Lettuce Wraps
■ Szechan Tofu with rice
■ Rice Noodle Salad with Oriental Vegetables
■ Lemon Grass Sorbet

MENU 2

A Summer Dinner Party:
■ Roast Pepper and Aubergine Mousse with melba toasts
■ Asparagus Fettucine Stir-fry with Peanut Sauce
■ Wild Flower and Herb Salad
■ Brandied Apricot Stacks

MENU 3

A Winter/Christmas menu:
■ Carrot Soup
■ Sweet and Sour Cabbage Parcels
■ Celeriac Mash
■ Steamed green vegetables of your choice (e.g. beans and broccoli)
■ Peach and Pear Compote with Cinnamon

GLOSSARY OF INGREDIENTS

AGAR AGAR

Also known as kanten or china grass, this sea vegetable is used as a vegetarian alternative to gelatine. Usually found in flaked or, occasionally, powdered form from a health food shop. Flakes are probably the best to use as they are processed using natural rather than chemical methods.

ARAME

This sea vegetable is rich in calcium and iodine. If you are unfamiliar with the taste and texture of sea vegetables, this is a good one to start with as it has a mild flavour and is softer in texture than some of the others. Being black in colour, it provides an excellent contrast in salads and stir-fries. Soak it for at least 5 minutes in warm water, or 10 minutes in cold, before using.

BUCKWHEAT

A gluten-free grain that has a strong, earthy flavour. You can buy raw whole buckwheat, roasted buckwheat (also known as kasha), buckwheat flour (traditionally used for crêpes in Brittany and blinis in Russia) or soba (buckwheat) noodles. Buckwheat contains rutin which is good for poor circulation.

CAPERS

Usually pickled in brine or packed in salt, with or without their leaves, these are the flower buds of a bush that grows around the Mediterranean. Capers have a strong and distinctive flavour and should be used sparingly or they will overpower a dish.

CELERIAC

A knobbly root vegetable with a strong, sweet celery flavour. Prepare it as you would a swede or turnip by peeling off the outer 'skin' and cutting the flesh into chunks. It can be boiled, steamed or fried, or roasted after parboiling. It's delicious boiled, then mashed with potatoes.

CEPS

Also known as porcini ('little pigs' in Italian) because of their shape. These are wild mushrooms, usually purchased in dried form. They need reconstituting before use. Ceps have a very rich, intense flavour and the dried mushrooms can be ground to a fine powder and added to soups or stews to enrich the flavours.

FETA CHEESE

This is a Greek cheese which is traditionally made from sheeps' milk although most sold commercially nowadays is made from cows' milk. It has quite a sour salty flavour and crumbly texture, and although it is good in salads, it is also useful in cooking as it doesn't lose its shape.

FROMAGE FRAIS

A soft cream cheese that varies between one and eight per cent fat content. It is usually thickened with a culture, and vegetarians should check the label on the carton to make sure that animal rennet has not been used. It is non-acidic and goes well with fruit. It is also useful in cooking, especially in soups and sauces, as it does not curdle if boiled.

GARAM MASALA

An Indian spice mixture. Although this can be bought ready mixed, you will obtain a better flavour by mixing your own selection of (seven) spices when required. Experiment until you find the mix of ingredients in the proportions that you like best.

GRANOLA

This is toasted muesli and tends to be higher in fat and sugar than muesli.

HIZIKI

Also spelt hijiki, this is a sun-dried and coarsely shredded sea vegetable from Japan. Hiziki translates as the 'bearer of wealth and beauty'. It is similar in appearance to arame but has a more chewy texture. It is rich in calcium, iron and fibre and should be soaked before use.

LEMON GRASS

A very distinctive ingredient in Thai and other South-east Asian cuisines, this fragrant herb has become widely available in the West. There is no substitute for the fresh lemon grass; in dried and powdered form, it is a pale shadow of the fresh flavour. If you are unable to obtain fresh lemon grass, substitute lemon zest instead. It can be used in both sweet and savoury dishes.

MAPLE SYRUP

This sweetening agent is obtained from the sap of the maple trees in Canada and North America. The sap is heated and concentrated to give a rich colour and flavour. It takes between 35–50 gallons of sap to make one gallon of syrup. Beware of cheap maple-flavoured syrups which may contain only two per cent maple syrup. It can be used as a substitute for honey in many dishes, which makes it a useful ingredient for anyone on a strict vegan diet.

MILLET

A gluten-free grain consisting of tiny, yellow, hulled balls. Millet has a very light texture when cooked and is high in iron, protein and the B group of vitamins. It can be used in place of rice in salads, bakes and risottos and should be cooked for about 15 minutes in three times the amount of water to grain. You can also buy millet flakes and millet flour.

MIRIN

This is a Japanese sweet cooking wine. It is always used for cooking and is never drunk by the glass. Mirin is made by fermenting yeasted rice grains over a period of about six months. It is used in oriental cooking to balance salty seasonings and to enhance the flavours of vinegared dishes, such as dressings, dips, sauces and glazes. If you are unable to obtain it, then a vegetarian sherry is the nearest substitute.

MISO

This savoury paste is formed by combining cooked soya beans with grains, yeasted grains and sea salt, which are then left to ferment for one to two years. It is rich in protein, B vitamins and minerals. Use sparingly as it is strongly flavoured, and blend with a little water or stock before adding to a soup or stew to ensure that it is properly mixed into the dish. It should be stored in a covered container in a cool place although it should not be necessary to refrigerate it. Sometimes a white yeast activity will be seen on the surface of the miso. This is not harmful and can be stirred back in. The most commonly found miso in this country is barley or mugi miso. You may also find genmai (kome) or rice miso, hatcho (no grain) miso, or sweet white miso.

MOLASSES

A by-product of sugar refining. It contains 50–70 per cent sucrose, the remainder being water and the nutrients form the original cane, plus calcium and iron from the processing which can be significant if iron vats are used for storing the product. Unsulphured blackstrap molasses is the best to buy. In ordinary molasses, traces of the sulphur used in the processing may remain; and Barbados molasses, which is made from cane juice which has been filtered and boiled, lacks the nutrient content of blackstrap.

MOOLI

Also known as daikon or white radish, this is an oriental member of the radish family. It looks like a very large, white, smooth parsnip and can be sliced and cooked in stir fries, or grated and eaten raw in a salad. It contains a high level of vitamin C.

PASSATA

Cooked and sieved tomatoes. Passata can usually be bought in a bottle or tetra pack and adds a lovely rich flavour to soups, stews or sauces, wherever a strong tomato flavour is required.

PINE NUTS OR KERNELS

These nuts have become very popular and, although expensive, can be used sparingly because of their strong flavour. Often better toasted, they can be used in salads, stir-fries, quiches, and to make pesto. They have a high oil content and should be refrigerated or frozen as they quickly become rancid.

QUARK

A soft, low-fat curd cheese which is traditionally made in Germany. It is very useful in sauces and in pâtés.

QUINOA

Pronounced 'keen-wah', this gluten-free grain is very useful in a vegetarian diet as it is an excellent source of protein. This is the sacred grain of the Incas, but is now grown in the UK. Use it wherever you would use rice or bulgar wheat. Cook for about 15 minutes in three times the amount of water to grain.

SAMBAL OELEK

Indonesian chilli paste. This is very hot so use sparingly.

SHOYU

A light soy sauce made by fermenting soya beans with sea salt and water and ageing for at least 18 months. Shoyu contains wheat and is therefore not suitable for anyone suffering from a wheat or gluten allergy. It has a lighter flavour than tamari.

SOURED CREAM

About 18 per cent fat content (the same as single cream), so use sparingly. Cream is pasteurized and homogenized and is then soured by the addition of a lactic acid starter culture. You can sour single cream with the addition of a little lemon juice, if preferred.

SOYA CREAM

A very useful non-dairy cream made from soya beans. It is similar in consistency to single cream and can be used as a substitute for cream, either stirred into dishes to give a creamy flavour and texture, or poured over desserts.

SPELT FLOUR

This grain is similar to wheat and originated in the Middle East. It was reintroduced to Britain fairly recently and is now grown on a commercial scale. It is extremely good for bread-making, being high in protein. It also appears to cause less problems for some sufferers of grain allergies. It is highly water-soluble and easy to digest. You can also buy spelt pasta.

SZECHUAN PEPPER

Also known as Sichuan pepper, fagara and anise pepper, this spice is not related to the black and white peppercorns with which we are familiar in Western cookery. Szechuan pepper is the red-brown berry of a Chinese ash tree. It is one of the constituents of Chinese five-spice powder.

TAHINI

Sesame seeds creamed with oil. Although it has a high fat content, the sesame seeds are a good source of calcium and zinc which cannot be accessed unless the seeds are crushed or creamed. Most commonly found in hummus, it also makes a delicious breakfast spread when mixed with a little yeast extract, and can be used to thicken soups and stews or to bind savoury loaves (e.g. nut loaf) in place of egg.

TAMARI

A dark soy sauce made by fermenting soya beans with sea salt and water and ageing for at least 18 months. Unlike shoyu, tamari is wheat-free and has a rich, deep flavour which is useful in soups, stews and stir-fries.

TERIYAKI

This is a tamari based marinating sauce with added ingredients, such as sweet rice wine, rice vinegar, plum juice and garlic. However, it is not usually suitable for anyone following a strict vegan diet as it usually contains honey.

TOFU

Tofu or bean curd is made from the humble soya bean. The beans are processed to make soya 'milk' which is then curdled, in a process similar to cheese-making, to produce tofu. It can be bought in firm blocks, which may be plain, smoked or marinated, and are good for savoury dishes, such as stir-fries, pâtés and stews, or in a softer form – 'silken' tofu – which is best used for desserts or as an egg and cream substitute in flans where a smoother, runnier texture is required. It is very high in protein, very low in saturated fats, low in carbohydrates, cholesterol-free and rich in calcium, vitamins and minerals.

WASABI

Also known as Japanese horseradish, this can be found in powdered or paste form in Chinese and Japanese supermarkets. It is even stronger than ordinary horseradish and should be added to dishes with care. It is usually used as a condiment with sushi and is bright green in colour.

INDEX

THE VEGETARIAN SOCIETY

The Vegetarian Society is the official voice of vegetarianism in the United Kingdon. The Society exists to promote Vegetarianism in the UK and throughout the world through research, national campaigns, education, liaison with the food industry and via our cookery school.

A registered charity established in 1847, the Society is the leading authority on vegetarian issues, providing expert information on the vegetarian diet, for the benefit of animal welfare, human health and the environment. The Society provides information and resources for use by the public, media, health professionals, schools and opinion formers.

Members of the Society receive a full-colour quarterly magazine full of the latest news, features and recipes, a discount card for use at hundreds of establishments, a unique seedling logo badge, access to our membership hotline and reduced rate subscription to *Wildlife* magazine. Membership support is vital to the Society's promotional and campaigning work. Members can become actively involved in the Society's work through the local group network or through the Council of Trustees, elected from the members.

The Society runs its own cookery school, Cordon Vert, the home of excellent vegetarian cuisine. The School runs inspirational courses to suit all abilities and interests from day courses through to a four-week Diploma course. Whatever your interest – Italian, Middle Eastern, Indian, Cajun or Thai cuisine – the Cordon Vert Cookery School has something to offer.

The Society works with major food manufacturers and retailers to improve the quality, quantity and variety of vegetarian food available, The Society also runs its own licence scheme, known as the seedling symbol, approving over 2,000 products which are guaranteed to be 100 per cent vegetarian.

The Vegetarian Society needs membership support if it is to continue to operate at all levels to spread the vegetarian message. For a free vegetarian starter pack or details of the Cordon Vert Cookery School, please call us on 0161 925 2000 or write to the address below:

The Vegetarian Society
Parkdale
Dunham Road
Altrincham
Cheshire WA14 4QG

E-Mail address is HYPERLINK mailto:info@vegsoc.org

Internet address: HYPERLINK http://www.vegsoc.org